Bicycling®

Training Journal

Name

_____

Address

_____

_____

Journal for the Year

_____ to _____

Bicycling®
TRAINING JOURNAL

A daily dose of motivation, training tips, and wisdom for every kind of cyclist—from fitness riders to competitive racers

By the Editors of *Bicycling* Magazine

RODALE

© 2004 by Rodale Inc.

Bicycling is a registered trademark of Rodale Inc.

Book design by Drew Frantzen
Photo Editor: Sarah Lee

ISBN 1–57954–935–7 paperback

Distributed to the book trade by St. Martin's Press

2   4   6   8   10   9   7   5   3   1   paperback

Visit us on the Web at www.bicycling.com,
or call us toll-free at (800) 848-4735.

WE **INSPIRE** AND **ENABLE** PEOPLE TO IMPROVE
THEIR LIVES AND THE WORLD AROUND THEM

CONTENTS

INTRODUCTION

B e careful—you're holding a training journal in your hands. That's right, *training*! Intervals and max heart rates. Climbing repeats and lactate thresholds. VO$_2$ max and all that scary-sounding stuff.

But here's the thing: This wonderful book isn't just about speed and sweat. It's about journaling, too. No matter how seriously or casually you're riding—whether you've sworn to lose weight, breeze through that upcoming charity ride, or, heck, to outright win a race this year (or even if you're just getting out a few times weekly to spin away stress)—you'll find great rewards in jotting a few notes about your adventures.

For instance: Thanks to my journal, I know that on May 22, 2002, I cruised for 91 minutes on the Thursday Night Loop. I was alone. I nearly ran over a tiny turtle sitting on the road's paint stripe, which reminded me of how my daughter used to call the shelled creatures "frogs" when she was younger. I also know that on January 11, 1999, I did a hill climb with my wife, Beth, that fried our brains bad; by the last ascent, Beth didn't realize she was in the big ring and kept complaining about how tired her legs were.

Even the stats I've kept tell a story. For the hill climb, which occurred during a happy period when I mostly rode around aimlessly, I know nothing more than that it was my 11th ride in a row, in what would become a string of 42. On the frog ride, when I was training to race, I know that my average heart rate was 139, that I peaked at 174 and spent 5 minutes above my lactate threshold, that the temperature was 52°F and that I must have been overtrained because my resting heart rate that morning was 68.

The diligent recording of training data helped me race strong that year, spotting peaks and avoiding mistakes. But being forever able to retrieve the fact that I almost ran over that turtle is just as fulfilling. Thanks to this book, you'll be able to do the same.

Enjoy your rides—and reading about them.

—*Bill Strickland*
  Executive Editor
  Bicycling *Magazine*

HOW TO USE THIS JOURNAL

IT'S MORE THAN JUST MILES.

Using a training journal might imply a certain level of seriousness, and in some ways that's exactly why we've created this book. Many happy cyclists are overjoyed to beat personal bests: climbing better, time-trialing faster, or simply riding 10 minutes longer. Others pedal to stay fit and look good. If these are your goals, you're in luck: There's no better way to get there than by logging and assessing your daily and weekly rides on these pages.

But we know "miles clocked" and "pounds shed" aren't the only reason you ride. You want to have fun—probably the reason why you started in the first place. You want the feeling of wind tugging on your jersey, the bursts of power popping from your quads, the wash of adrenaline that lingers long after a ride has finished.

Don't be afraid to use your *Bicycling Training Journal* to capture that fun. Just don't forget to keep consistent track of a few details. Recording some basic facts (mileage, where you rode, et cetera) will help you stay focused on the goals you've set and what you've accomplished. Then, if you want to fill the page with a sweat-soaked story about how gritty and fun a particular ride was, it's entirely your call.

Above all else, remember: Enjoy the ride.

GOALS

GOOD INTENTION ALONE WILL GET YOU NO PLACE; FOCUS YOUR MOTIVATION HERE.

There are as many reasons to keep this journal as there are riders. Maybe you're inching your way, step-by-step, into Tour de France contention (or small, local race glory). Perhaps you vowed to cover every trail on the mountain near your home. Or maybe your goal is the noblest in all of cycling: teaching a child to ride.

Ultimately, it doesn't matter what motivates you—only that you're motivated. Keeping a running set of goals is a great way to ensure you're advancing, improving, and making the most of your hours on the pedals. Remember, these goals are for you, so keep them personal and creative. Most important, make sure they're attainable. Nothing's more frustrating than continued failure. We encourage you to make short-, medium-, and long-term goals. Place the greatest emphasis on attaining the short-term goals, but dare to aim for those that seem a long way off. And don't forget to update and change your list as much as is necessary. Setting goals, like cycling, is anything but static. Get going.

GOALS

_____

_____

_____

_____

_____

_____

_____

_____

_____

_____

_____

_____

_____

_____

_____

_____

_____

_____

_____

_____

_____

_____

_____

_____

_____

_____

_____

_____

_____

_____

_____

"Nothing compares to the simple pleasure of a bike ride."

—*John F. Kennedy*

Fix a Flat Fast

To fix a flat fast remember these three things: For most tires you don't need tire levers. Work the tire off with your bare hands starting in the area opposite of the valve. A tube that has enough air in it to give it some shape goes in more easily. Always check the bead of the tire when you have about 25 psi pumped into it. You'll want to make sure there are no high or low spots.

MONDAY

GOAL: ☐

ROUTE:

DISTANCE/TIME:

WEATHER CONDITIONS:

THOUGHTS:

TUESDAY

GOAL: ☐

ROUTE:

DISTANCE/TIME:

WEATHER CONDITIONS:

THOUGHTS:

WEDNESDAY

GOAL: ☐

ROUTE:

DISTANCE/TIME:

WEATHER CONDITIONS:

THOUGHTS:

THURSDAY

GOAL: ☐

ROUTE:

DISTANCE/TIME:

WEATHER CONDITIONS:

THOUGHTS:

FRIDAY

GOAL: ☐

ROUTE:

DISTANCE/TIME:

WEATHER CONDITIONS:

THOUGHTS:

SATURDAY

GOAL: ☐

ROUTE:

DISTANCE/TIME:

WEATHER CONDITIONS:

THOUGHTS:

SUNDAY

GOAL: ☐

ROUTE:

DISTANCE/TIME:

WEATHER CONDITIONS:

THOUGHTS:

TIP OF THE WEEK

Consistent Mileage

The key for new riders is logging consistent saddle time. You can begin building endurance and acclimating your body to the bike with rides as short as 15 to 20 minutes. Simple jaunts around the block are better than nothing.

WEEKLY TOTAL

TOTAL MILEAGE TO DATE

"Everybody wants to know what I'm on. What am I on? I'm on my bike busting my ass 6 hours a day. What are you on?"

—*Lance Armstrong*

TIP OF THE WEEK

Getting Back in the Saddle?

After a long layoff, try riding 15 minutes every day for 1 week. The next week, cut back to 4 or 5 days but increase each session to 20 to 30 minutes if possible.

MONDAY

GOAL: ☐

ROUTE:

DISTANCE/TIME:

WEATHER CONDITIONS:

THOUGHTS:

TUESDAY

GOAL: ☐

ROUTE:

DISTANCE/TIME:

WEATHER CONDITIONS:

THOUGHTS:

WEDNESDAY

GOAL: ☐

ROUTE:

DISTANCE/TIME:

WEATHER CONDITIONS:

THOUGHTS:

THURSDAY

GOAL: ☐

ROUTE:

DISTANCE/TIME:

WEATHER CONDITIONS:

THOUGHTS:

FRIDAY

GOAL: ☐

ROUTE:

DISTANCE/TIME:

WEATHER CONDITIONS:

THOUGHTS:

SATURDAY

GOAL: ☐

ROUTE:

DISTANCE/TIME:

WEATHER CONDITIONS:

THOUGHTS:

SUNDAY

GOAL: ☐

ROUTE:

DISTANCE/TIME:

WEATHER CONDITIONS:

THOUGHTS:

WEEKLY TOTAL

TOTAL MILEAGE TO DATE

Prevent Flat Tires

Want to ensure that you won't flat? Here's how:

1. **Dust your tubes with talcum powder:** A light coat of talcum powder will keep the tube from becoming stuck against the inside of your tire and will decrease the chance of a pinch-flat.

2. **Slime 'em:** Inject a puncture-resistant solution such as Slime into your tubes. It adds weight (roughly 50 to 100 grams per wheel) but makes your tires nearly flat-proof.

3. **Go tubeless:** Try a tubeless system. Because there's no tube, you can't pinch flat. Tubeless tires use slightly thicker rubber, meaning you're not likely to have a flat from a puncture.

"The bicycle is the most civilized conveyance known to man. Other forms of transport grow daily more nightmarish. Only the bicycle remains pure in heart."

—*author Iris Murdoch,*
   The Red and the Green

Lube Your Chain

Have your chain roughly in the middle of your cassette and, as you pedal backward, put a drop of oil on every other link. After you've gone around the entire chain, pick up a shop rag and, still pedaling backward, spread the lube evenly across all the links. Remove all excess. It shouldn't take more than a minute.

MONDAY

GOAL: ☐

ROUTE:

DISTANCE/TIME:

WEATHER CONDITIONS:

THOUGHTS:

TUESDAY

GOAL: ☐

ROUTE:

DISTANCE/TIME:

WEATHER CONDITIONS:

THOUGHTS:

WEDNESDAY

GOAL: ☐

ROUTE:

DISTANCE/TIME:

WEATHER CONDITIONS:

THOUGHTS:

THURSDAY

GOAL: ☐

ROUTE:

DISTANCE/TIME:

WEATHER CONDITIONS:

THOUGHTS:

FRIDAY

GOAL: ☐

ROUTE:

DISTANCE/TIME:

WEATHER CONDITIONS:

THOUGHTS:

SATURDAY

GOAL: ☐

ROUTE:

DISTANCE/TIME:

WEATHER CONDITIONS:

THOUGHTS:

SUNDAY

GOAL: ☐

ROUTE:

DISTANCE/TIME:

WEATHER CONDITIONS:

THOUGHTS:

WEEKLY TOTAL

TOTAL MILEAGE TO DATE

TIP OF THE WEEK

Stay Active

After a big ride, active recovery is generally better than taking a day off. A brisk walk, a short spin, or a yoga class—anything that works your body without stressing it—is great for recovery.

"Machines don't break records. Muscles do."

—*Lon Haldeman, famed long-distance rider*

Wash Your Bike in 15 Minutes

Fill a bucket with cold, soapy water. Pop both wheels off your bike. Grab your frame and, starting from the top down, wash with a sponge, taking care to hit hard-to-reach areas. Then rinse the frame with cold water and dry with a rag. Next, grab your front wheel, scrubbing the hub first and working your way out to the tire. Do the same for the back wheel, hitting the cassette last. Rinse both wheels and dry. Finally, reassemble the bike, lubing the chain and other important moving parts.

MONDAY
GOAL: ☐

ROUTE:

DISTANCE/TIME:

WEATHER CONDITIONS:

THOUGHTS:

TUESDAY
GOAL: ☐

ROUTE:

DISTANCE/TIME:

WEATHER CONDITIONS:

THOUGHTS:

WEDNESDAY
GOAL: ☐

ROUTE:

DISTANCE/TIME:

WEATHER CONDITIONS:

THOUGHTS:

THURSDAY
GOAL: ☐

ROUTE:

DISTANCE/TIME:

WEATHER CONDITIONS:

THOUGHTS:

FRIDAY

GOAL: ☐

ROUTE:

DISTANCE/TIME:

WEATHER CONDITIONS:

THOUGHTS:

SATURDAY

GOAL: ☐

ROUTE:

DISTANCE/TIME:

WEATHER CONDITIONS:

THOUGHTS:

SUNDAY

GOAL: ☐

ROUTE:

DISTANCE/TIME:

WEATHER CONDITIONS:

THOUGHTS:

TIP OF THE WEEK

Missed Workout?

You want to follow your training plan as closely as you can, but count on missing some workouts because of bad weather, work, school, or family commitments. If you miss a workout, don't toss the entire week. What's important is your overall effort. Training plans are suggestions, not commandments.

WEEKLY TOTAL

TOTAL MILEAGE TO DATE

"I'm going again."

—Graeme Obree upon hearing that he missed breaking the hour record by two-tenths of a mile. Obree broke the record the next day. (For comparison, legendary cycling champ Eddy Merckx was reportedly bedridden for a week after his successful hour record ride.)

Tape Your Bars

Cut two 4-inch pieces of electrical tape and hang them from the top tube of your bike. Fold your brake hoods away from the bar and peel the old tape off your bars. Grab a roll of fresh tape and wrap from the bottom, making sure to keep constant pressure on the tape. At the junction of the brake lever, make a figure eight around the lever and continue wrapping. Two inches from the edge of the stem, cut the bar tape and finish it off with one of the pieces of electrical tape that you stuck on your top tube. Repeat on the remaining side of the bars.

MONDAY
GOAL: ☐
ROUTE:
DISTANCE/TIME:
WEATHER CONDITIONS:
THOUGHTS:

TUESDAY
GOAL: ☐
ROUTE:
DISTANCE/TIME:
WEATHER CONDITIONS:
THOUGHTS:

WEDNESDAY
GOAL: ☐
ROUTE:
DISTANCE/TIME:
WEATHER CONDITIONS:
THOUGHTS:

THURSDAY
GOAL: ☐
ROUTE:
DISTANCE/TIME:
WEATHER CONDITIONS:
THOUGHTS:

FRIDAY
GOAL: ☐

ROUTE:

DISTANCE/TIME:

WEATHER CONDITIONS:

THOUGHTS:

SATURDAY
GOAL: ☐

ROUTE:

DISTANCE/TIME:

WEATHER CONDITIONS:

THOUGHTS:

SUNDAY
GOAL: ☐

ROUTE:

DISTANCE/TIME:

WEATHER CONDITIONS:

THOUGHTS:

WEEKLY TOTAL

TOTAL MILEAGE TO DATE

TIP OF THE WEEK

Riding with a Significant Beginner

If you're riding with a beginner, let the beginner lead and set the pace. Let the beginner decide when to rest and when to quit. If this beginner is your significant other, your life depends on this.

> "Whatever
> the goal
> undertaken,
> the road always
> leads upwards
> and on."

—*Ernesto Colnago, famed
equipment supplier to
thousands of professional
racers, including Eddy
Merckx, winner of five
Tours de France, five
Tours of Italy, and three
World Championships*

Dry Your Shoes

After a wet ride, the best way to dry your shoes is to stuff them with wadded newspaper. The paper will pull the water from the soggy material and help your shoes maintain the proper shape. Remove the paper after 8 to 10 hours. Repeat if necessary.

MONDAY

GOAL: ☐

ROUTE:

DISTANCE/TIME:

WEATHER CONDITIONS:

THOUGHTS:

TUESDAY

GOAL: ☐

ROUTE:

DISTANCE/TIME:

WEATHER CONDITIONS:

THOUGHTS:

WEDNESDAY

GOAL: ☐

ROUTE:

DISTANCE/TIME:

WEATHER CONDITIONS:

THOUGHTS:

THURSDAY

GOAL: ☐

ROUTE:

DISTANCE/TIME:

WEATHER CONDITIONS:

THOUGHTS:

FRIDAY

GOAL: ☐

ROUTE:

DISTANCE/TIME:

WEATHER CONDITIONS:

THOUGHTS:

SATURDAY

GOAL: ☐

ROUTE:

DISTANCE/TIME:

WEATHER CONDITIONS:

THOUGHTS:

SUNDAY

GOAL: ☐

ROUTE:

DISTANCE/TIME:

WEATHER CONDITIONS:

THOUGHTS:

TIP OF THE WEEK

Better Makes Best

At least once a week, ride with a group that includes cyclists who are better than you. Stronger riders push you harder than you'd push yourself. You'll make a quantum leap in your speed, endurance, and confidence.

WEEKLY TOTAL

TOTAL MILEAGE TO DATE

"I never raced to break records. I raced to enjoy myself."

—five-time Tour de France winner Bernard Hinault

MONDAY

GOAL: ☐

ROUTE:

DISTANCE/TIME:

WEATHER CONDITIONS:

THOUGHTS:

TUESDAY

GOAL: ☐

ROUTE:

DISTANCE/TIME:

WEATHER CONDITIONS:

THOUGHTS:

Lose 5 Pounds in 5 Weeks

Cut 500 calories per day from your diet and you'll drop a pound a week. Start by targeting sweet foods and alcohol; they stimulate the overproduction of insulin, which makes you crave even more food and promotes the storage of fat, even if you're on a low-calorie diet.

WEDNESDAY

GOAL: ☐

ROUTE:

DISTANCE/TIME:

WEATHER CONDITIONS:

THOUGHTS:

THURSDAY

GOAL: ☐

ROUTE:

DISTANCE/TIME:

WEATHER CONDITIONS:

THOUGHTS:

FRIDAY

GOAL: ☐

ROUTE:

DISTANCE/TIME:

WEATHER CONDITIONS:

THOUGHTS:

SATURDAY

GOAL: ☐

ROUTE:

DISTANCE/TIME:

WEATHER CONDITIONS:

THOUGHTS:

SUNDAY

GOAL: ☐

ROUTE:

DISTANCE/TIME:

WEATHER CONDITIONS:

THOUGHTS:

WEEKLY TOTAL

TOTAL MILEAGE TO DATE

TIP OF THE WEEK

Endurance Training

Endurance rides are long, steady efforts at an aerobic level (60 to 85 percent of your maximum heart rate). They are especially helpful for new riders, because their bodies have to learn how to burn fat when they're depleted of glycogen.

"I need to go out and have a good time every couple weeks, go to the movies, and play golf once a week or something. I do that because I know it's going to add to my cycling."

—three-time Tour de France champion Greg LeMond

Train like a Rock Star

Athletes are only human; they need to enjoy life like the rest of us. The key to having a good time at the bars tonight and still being able to train hard tomorrow is to eat a big meal before you hit the booze. Once you do, stick with gin or vodka, as they have the least fermentation by-products and burn the cleanest. You should also down one glass of water for every drink and have one big glass of water and two aspirins just before you get in bed.

MONDAY

GOAL: ☐

ROUTE:

DISTANCE/TIME:

WEATHER CONDITIONS:

THOUGHTS:

TUESDAY

GOAL: ☐

ROUTE:

DISTANCE/TIME:

WEATHER CONDITIONS:

THOUGHTS:

WEDNESDAY

GOAL: ☐

ROUTE:

DISTANCE/TIME:

WEATHER CONDITIONS:

THOUGHTS:

THURSDAY

GOAL: ☐

ROUTE:

DISTANCE/TIME:

WEATHER CONDITIONS:

THOUGHTS:

FRIDAY

GOAL: ☐

ROUTE:

DISTANCE/TIME:

WEATHER CONDITIONS:

THOUGHTS:

SATURDAY

GOAL: ☐

ROUTE:

DISTANCE/TIME:

WEATHER CONDITIONS:

THOUGHTS:

SUNDAY

GOAL: ☐

ROUTE:

DISTANCE/TIME:

WEATHER CONDITIONS:

THOUGHTS:

WEEKLY TOTAL

TOTAL MILEAGE TO DATE

TIP OF THE WEEK

Learn to layer according to the weather.
First layer: light, snuggy fabrics that wick. This can be bike shorts, a jersey, or some kind of polypro shirt and long johns.
Middle layer: insulators that trap warmth but still transport your sweat outward.
Outer layer: a barrier to keep the elements out. Anything from a wind-repellent jacket to a full-on Gore-Tex suit of armor.

"To be afraid is a priceless education."

—*Lance Armstrong*

Find a Good Coach

Cycling's governing body in America, USA Cycling, has a licensing and certification program that ensures the quality of the coaches that it sanctions. Regardless of certification level—USA Cycling has three—the best coach for you is one who fits your style and can help you develop into a more complete cyclist, by teaching skills, strategy, tactics, nutrition, et cetera. You can find a listing of all USA Cycling certified coaches at www.bicyclecoach.com.

MONDAY
GOAL: ☐

ROUTE:

DISTANCE/TIME:

WEATHER CONDITIONS:

THOUGHTS:

TUESDAY
GOAL: ☐

ROUTE:

DISTANCE/TIME:

WEATHER CONDITIONS:

THOUGHTS:

WEDNESDAY
GOAL: ☐

ROUTE:

DISTANCE/TIME:

WEATHER CONDITIONS:

THOUGHTS:

THURSDAY
GOAL: ☐

ROUTE:

DISTANCE/TIME:

WEATHER CONDITIONS:

THOUGHTS:

FRIDAY

GOAL: ☐

ROUTE:

DISTANCE/TIME:

WEATHER CONDITIONS:

THOUGHTS:

SATURDAY

GOAL: ☐

ROUTE:

DISTANCE/TIME:

WEATHER CONDITIONS:

THOUGHTS:

SUNDAY

GOAL: ☐

ROUTE:

DISTANCE/TIME:

WEATHER CONDITIONS:

THOUGHTS:

TIP OF THE WEEK

Far from the Usual

Travel will make you a complete rider. If you're an eastern-style pick-and-poke rider, plan a vacation on super-fast buff stuff. Go to the big altitude if you're a flatlander. And if you're one of those gifted souls who lives in a mountain bike mecca, explore the singletrack in a place like Alabama.

WEEKLY TOTAL

TOTAL MILEAGE TO DATE

"Bicycle racing
has two kinds
of winners,
those who win
races and those
who win our
hearts."

—author James Startt,
Tour de France/Tour de
Force

Treat a Poisonous Snake Bite

Clean the wound with clean water. Slow the flow of venom by immobilizing the area around the bite and by keeping it lower than your heart. If it's going to be more than 20 minutes until you can get to a doctor, use a jersey or other piece of cloth as a tourniquet. Place it just above the wound, keeping it loose enough that a finger can fit between the tourniquet and your skin. Get to a doctor as soon as possible, even if you don't believe the venom is poisonous.

MONDAY

GOAL: ☐

ROUTE:

DISTANCE/TIME:

WEATHER CONDITIONS:

THOUGHTS:

TUESDAY

GOAL: ☐

ROUTE:

DISTANCE/TIME:

WEATHER CONDITIONS:

THOUGHTS:

WEDNESDAY

GOAL: ☐

ROUTE:

DISTANCE/TIME:

WEATHER CONDITIONS:

THOUGHTS:

THURSDAY

GOAL: ☐

ROUTE:

DISTANCE/TIME:

WEATHER CONDITIONS:

THOUGHTS:

FRIDAY

GOAL: ☐

ROUTE:

DISTANCE/TIME:

WEATHER CONDITIONS:

THOUGHTS:

SATURDAY

GOAL: ☐

ROUTE:

DISTANCE/TIME:

WEATHER CONDITIONS:

THOUGHTS:

SUNDAY

GOAL: ☐

ROUTE:

DISTANCE/TIME:

WEATHER CONDITIONS:

THOUGHTS:

WEEKLY TOTAL

TOTAL MILEAGE TO DATE

TIP OF THE WEEK

Packing for a Trip?

• Always make a list of things to take and check it twice.
• You need twice as many socks and inner tubes as you think.
• Pack arm warmers and leave your long-sleeve jerseys at home.
• Pack your favorite type of energy bar or gel. They might not have it where you're going.

"Anything is possible. You can be told that you have a 90 percent chance or a 50 percent chance or a 1 percent chance, but you have to believe, and you have to fight."

—*Lance Armstrong*

Make Your Own Energy Gel

An average packet of energy gel yields 80 to 100 calories and 20 to 25 grams of carbohydrate. Quality gels include simple sugars such as fructose and long-chain carbohydrate/glucose polymers such as maltodextrin. Roughly the same amount of Karo Light Corn Syrup has 120 calories and 31 grams of carbohydrate. Add your favorite natural flavoring, such as vanilla or orange, pour it in a reusable plastic flask, and you're off.

MONDAY
GOAL:

ROUTE:

DISTANCE/TIME:

WEATHER CONDITIONS:

THOUGHTS:

TUESDAY
GOAL:

ROUTE:

DISTANCE/TIME:

WEATHER CONDITIONS:

THOUGHTS:

WEDNESDAY
GOAL:

ROUTE:

DISTANCE/TIME:

WEATHER CONDITIONS:

THOUGHTS:

THURSDAY
GOAL:

ROUTE:

DISTANCE/TIME:

WEATHER CONDITIONS:

THOUGHTS:

FRIDAY

GOAL: ☐

ROUTE:

DISTANCE/TIME:

WEATHER CONDITIONS:

THOUGHTS:

SATURDAY

GOAL: ☐

ROUTE:

DISTANCE/TIME:

WEATHER CONDITIONS:

THOUGHTS:

SUNDAY

GOAL: ☐

ROUTE:

DISTANCE/TIME:

WEATHER CONDITIONS:

THOUGHTS:

WEEKLY TOTAL

TOTAL MILEAGE TO DATE

TIP OF THE WEEK

Nothing Beats Experience

If you have a friend who knows bikes better than you, bring him or her along when you shop. You probably won't be able to arrange a real test ride (at least not on dirt), so try to find people who are already riding your top choices and get their input.

"Suffering is the sole origin of consciousness."

—*Fyodor Dostoyevsky*

Eat Junk and Still Fly

You're out on a ride and the only convenience store in sight hasn't heard of energy bars or even fresh fruit. What's the next best choice? If you have to eat junk food on a ride, go with Twinkies. One of the spongy, brown cakes has 150 calories, just 5 grams of fat (2 grams of saturated fat), 14 grams of sugar, and 20 milligrams of cholesterol. Sure, it's not an organic tofu and wheatgrass smoothie, but a pair of Twinkies will get you home in a pinch.

MONDAY

GOAL: ☐

ROUTE:

DISTANCE/TIME:

WEATHER CONDITIONS:

THOUGHTS:

TUESDAY

GOAL: ☐

ROUTE:

DISTANCE/TIME:

WEATHER CONDITIONS:

THOUGHTS:

WEDNESDAY

GOAL: ☐

ROUTE:

DISTANCE/TIME:

WEATHER CONDITIONS:

THOUGHTS:

THURSDAY

GOAL: ☐

ROUTE:

DISTANCE/TIME:

WEATHER CONDITIONS:

THOUGHTS:

FRIDAY

GOAL: ☐

ROUTE: _____

DISTANCE/TIME: _____

WEATHER CONDITIONS: _____

THOUGHTS: _____

SATURDAY

GOAL: ☐

ROUTE: _____

DISTANCE/TIME: _____

WEATHER CONDITIONS: _____

THOUGHTS: _____

SUNDAY

GOAL: ☐

ROUTE: _____

DISTANCE/TIME: _____

WEATHER CONDITIONS: _____

THOUGHTS: _____

TIP OF THE WEEK

Service Beats All

The most important element to look for in a shop—more important than slick displays, cut-rate prices, or all the latest accessories—is service. A staff that knows bikes, loves bikes, lives bikes—and that will talk to any customer with no attitude—deserves your business.

WEEKLY TOTAL

_____

TOTAL MILEAGE TO DATE

_____

"I did everything to win races, but without luck, I wouldn't be where I am."

—*Irishman Stephen Roche, who was the last rider to win the Tour of Italy, the Tour de France, and the World Road Championship in the same season*

Avoid a Bladder Infection

Spoon some baking soda, water, and rice into your hydration bladder, then close and shake for 2 minutes. The abrasiveness of the rice will scour the inside spotless while the baking soda disinfects and sanitizes.

MONDAY

GOAL: ☐

ROUTE:

DISTANCE/TIME:

WEATHER CONDITIONS:

THOUGHTS:

TUESDAY

GOAL: ☐

ROUTE:

DISTANCE/TIME:

WEATHER CONDITIONS:

THOUGHTS:

WEDNESDAY

GOAL: ☐

ROUTE:

DISTANCE/TIME:

WEATHER CONDITIONS:

THOUGHTS:

THURSDAY

GOAL: ☐

ROUTE:

DISTANCE/TIME:

WEATHER CONDITIONS:

THOUGHTS:

FRIDAY

GOAL: ☐

ROUTE: _____

DISTANCE/TIME: _____

WEATHER CONDITIONS: _____

THOUGHTS: _____

SATURDAY

GOAL: ☐

ROUTE: _____

DISTANCE/TIME: _____

WEATHER CONDITIONS: _____

THOUGHTS: _____

SUNDAY

GOAL: ☐

ROUTE: _____

DISTANCE/TIME: _____

WEATHER CONDITIONS: _____

THOUGHTS: _____

_____

TIP OF THE WEEK

Gas Up

Many new riders think they're not fit when all they really lack is energy. Low fuel can give you leg cramps, lousy concentration, bad mojo, and other ills. Keep yourself fed and watered and you can pedal beyond, your artificial boundaries.

WEEKLY TOTAL

_____

TOTAL MILEAGE TO DATE

_____

"An American in cycling was comparable to a French baseball team in the World Series. I was a gate-crasher in a revered and time-honored sport, and I had no concept of its rules, written and unwritten, or its etiquette. Let's just say that my Texas manners didn't play well on the continent."

—*Lance Armstrong*

MONDAY

GOAL: ☐

ROUTE:

DISTANCE/TIME:

WEATHER CONDITIONS:

THOUGHTS:

TUESDAY

GOAL: ☐

ROUTE:

DISTANCE/TIME:

WEATHER CONDITIONS:

THOUGHTS:

WEDNESDAY

GOAL: ☐

ROUTE:

DISTANCE/TIME:

WEATHER CONDITIONS:

THOUGHTS:

THURSDAY

GOAL: ☐

ROUTE:

DISTANCE/TIME:

WEATHER CONDITIONS:

THOUGHTS:

FRIDAY

GOAL: ☐

ROUTE: _____

DISTANCE/TIME: _____

WEATHER CONDITIONS: _____

THOUGHTS: _____

SATURDAY

GOAL: ☐

ROUTE: _____

DISTANCE/TIME: _____

WEATHER CONDITIONS: _____

THOUGHTS: _____

SUNDAY

GOAL: ☐

ROUTE: _____

DISTANCE/TIME: _____

WEATHER CONDITIONS: _____

THOUGHTS: _____

_____

WEEKLY TOTAL

_____

TOTAL MILEAGE TO DATE

_____

TIP OF THE WEEK

Mother Knows Best

Gels, goos, bars, and mixes are never a bad idea, but bananas have no fat, with lots of carbohydrates and potassium to help balance your fluid level. Did we mention they're cheap and come directly from Mother Earth herself?

Make Bikes Matter

The quickest, easiest way to boost bike advocacy: Call the congressional switchboard (202-224-3121), ask to be transferred to your congressman's office, then tell them that you support the idea of more funding for U.S. Forest Service trails. That's it. The switchboard will even tell you who your senators and representatives are if you don't know.

"Eat before you are hungry. Drink before you are thirsty. Rest before you are tired. Cover up before you are cold. Peel off before you are hot. Don't drink or smoke on tour. Never ride just to prove yourself."

—*Paul de Vivie (a.k.a. Velocio), early advocate of the derailleur and 19th-century cycling journalist*

Check Your Chain

A dirty, stretched chain will ruin the rest of your drivetrain, so check your chain for wear every 1,000 miles or 6 months. Put it on the big chainring, then try to pull a single link off the ring. If you can see light between the chain and the ring, it's time for a new chain. Or purchase a chain-checking tool from Park or Rolhoff.

MONDAY

GOAL: ☐

ROUTE:

DISTANCE/TIME:

WEATHER CONDITIONS:

THOUGHTS:

TUESDAY

GOAL: ☐

ROUTE:

DISTANCE/TIME:

WEATHER CONDITIONS:

THOUGHTS:

WEDNESDAY

GOAL: ☐

ROUTE:

DISTANCE/TIME:

WEATHER CONDITIONS:

THOUGHTS:

THURSDAY

GOAL: ☐

ROUTE:

DISTANCE/TIME:

WEATHER CONDITIONS:

THOUGHTS:

FRIDAY

GOAL: ☐

ROUTE:

DISTANCE/TIME:

WEATHER CONDITIONS:

THOUGHTS:

SATURDAY

GOAL: ☐

ROUTE:

DISTANCE/TIME:

WEATHER CONDITIONS:

THOUGHTS:

SUNDAY

GOAL: ☐

ROUTE:

DISTANCE/TIME:

WEATHER CONDITIONS:

THOUGHTS:

WEEKLY TOTAL

TOTAL MILEAGE TO DATE

TIP OF THE WEEK

Drinking Habit

Sip your bottle or CamelBak once at least every 10 minutes and at the top of most hills. If you wait until you're thirsty, you'll never catch up. As long as you have a good supply of water, you can never drink too much.

"It never gets
easier, you just
go faster."

—Greg LeMond

Fix a Flat with No Spare

Got a flat, but no spare tube and no patches? No problem. Rip the tube apart at the puncture, then tie the ends into a tight knot and inflate. Although the ride will be bumpy, you'll be able to inflate the tube enough to get home. (You might have to refill the tube periodically.)

MONDAY
GOAL: ☐

ROUTE:

DISTANCE/TIME:

WEATHER CONDITIONS:

THOUGHTS:

TUESDAY
GOAL: ☐

ROUTE:

DISTANCE/TIME:

WEATHER CONDITIONS:

THOUGHTS:

WEDNESDAY
GOAL: ☐

ROUTE:

DISTANCE/TIME:

WEATHER CONDITIONS:

THOUGHTS:

THURSDAY
GOAL: ☐

ROUTE:

DISTANCE/TIME:

WEATHER CONDITIONS:

THOUGHTS:

FRIDAY

GOAL: ☐

ROUTE:

DISTANCE/TIME:

WEATHER CONDITIONS:

THOUGHTS:

SATURDAY

GOAL: ☐

ROUTE:

DISTANCE/TIME:

WEATHER CONDITIONS:

THOUGHTS:

SUNDAY

GOAL: ☐

ROUTE:

DISTANCE/TIME:

WEATHER CONDITIONS:

THOUGHTS:

TIP OF THE WEEK

Meal Plan

If you're going to be riding for more than 90 minutes, put yourself on a food schedule to ensure you don't bonk. Begin eating after just 30 minutes and eat something small (a gel or half an energy bar) every 20 minutes after that.

WEEKLY TOTAL

TOTAL MILEAGE TO DATE

"I always had and I still have that special desire in me to be the best. . . . That's why I accept, and that's why I am proud of the nickname that they once gave me."

—*Eddy Merckx, known as The Cannibal.*

Keep Suspension Smooth

Every time you lube the chain on your mountain bike, lube the seals on your shock and suspension fork. Apply the lube, push up and down on the suspension a half-dozen times, and wipe excess lube from the seals.

MONDAY

GOAL: ☐

ROUTE:

DISTANCE/TIME:

WEATHER CONDITIONS:

THOUGHTS:

TUESDAY

GOAL: ☐

ROUTE:

DISTANCE/TIME:

WEATHER CONDITIONS:

THOUGHTS:

WEDNESDAY

GOAL: ☐

ROUTE:

DISTANCE/TIME:

WEATHER CONDITIONS:

THOUGHTS:

THURSDAY

GOAL: ☐

ROUTE:

DISTANCE/TIME:

WEATHER CONDITIONS:

THOUGHTS:

FRIDAY

GOAL: ☐

ROUTE: _____

DISTANCE/TIME: _____

WEATHER CONDITIONS: _____

THOUGHTS: _____

SATURDAY

GOAL: ☐

ROUTE: _____

DISTANCE/TIME: _____

WEATHER CONDITIONS: _____

THOUGHTS: _____

SUNDAY

GOAL: ☐

ROUTE: _____

DISTANCE/TIME: _____

WEATHER CONDITIONS: _____

THOUGHTS: _____

TIP OF THE WEEK

Saddle Up?

Most riders prefer a level saddle, but some (including many women) find a slight nose-down tilt avoids pressure and irritation. Others go slightly nose up, which helps them sit back and reduce strain on their arms. The best way to determine what's right for you is to experiment.

WEEKLY TOTAL

_____

TOTAL MILEAGE TO DATE

_____

"The bicycle is a curious vehicle. Its passenger is its engine."

—American road racer John Howard

MONDAY
GOAL: ☐

ROUTE:

DISTANCE/TIME:

WEATHER CONDITIONS:

THOUGHTS:

TUESDAY
GOAL: ☐

ROUTE:

DISTANCE/TIME:

WEATHER CONDITIONS:

THOUGHTS:

Wanna Buy Some Duct?

On a bike there are a million ways duct tape can come in handy. Wrap a 4-inch-long piece around your seatpost so you're never without it.

WEDNESDAY
GOAL: ☐

ROUTE:

DISTANCE/TIME:

WEATHER CONDITIONS:

THOUGHTS:

THURSDAY
GOAL: ☐

ROUTE:

DISTANCE/TIME:

WEATHER CONDITIONS:

THOUGHTS:

FRIDAY

GOAL: ☐

ROUTE:

DISTANCE/TIME:

WEATHER CONDITIONS:

THOUGHTS:

SATURDAY

GOAL: ☐

ROUTE:

DISTANCE/TIME:

WEATHER CONDITIONS:

THOUGHTS:

SUNDAY

GOAL: ☐

ROUTE:

DISTANCE/TIME:

WEATHER CONDITIONS:

THOUGHTS:

TIP OF THE WEEK

Fore

Fore/aft saddle position is not for adjusting your reach to the handlebar— it's to find the position with the best mix of power and efficiency. Riders who specialize in climbing sometimes put their saddles farther forward so they can sit on the comfortable part of the seat rather than the narrow nose while climbing.

WEEKLY TOTAL

TOTAL MILEAGE TO DATE

"There is almost nothing in human creation more efficient, beautiful or perfect than a bicycle."

—*mountain bike pioneer, innovator, and entrepreneur Joe Breeze*

Keep Your Bike Shifting Smoothly

The best way to improve the shifting on your bike is to slap on a new chain. Old chains not only shift poorly but also cause cassettes and chainrings to wear more quickly. Replacing a $15 chain every 6 months is cheaper than replacing your entire drivetrain every 2 years.

MONDAY

GOAL:

ROUTE:

DISTANCE/TIME:

WEATHER CONDITIONS:

THOUGHTS:

TUESDAY

GOAL:

ROUTE:

DISTANCE/TIME:

WEATHER CONDITIONS:

THOUGHTS:

WEDNESDAY

GOAL:

ROUTE:

DISTANCE/TIME:

WEATHER CONDITIONS:

THOUGHTS:

THURSDAY

GOAL:

ROUTE:

DISTANCE/TIME:

WEATHER CONDITIONS:

THOUGHTS:

FRIDAY

GOAL: ☐

ROUTE:

DISTANCE/TIME:

WEATHER CONDITIONS:

THOUGHTS:

SATURDAY

GOAL: ☐

ROUTE:

DISTANCE/TIME:

WEATHER CONDITIONS:

THOUGHTS:

SUNDAY

GOAL: ☐

ROUTE:

DISTANCE/TIME:

WEATHER CONDITIONS:

THOUGHTS:

WEEKLY TOTAL

TOTAL MILEAGE TO DATE

TIP OF THE WEEK

Arm Absorbers

Relaxed and slightly bent arms act as shock absorbers. If you can only reach the bar with elbows locked, get a shorter stem and/or condition yourself to lean forward more. If your upper arms and shoulders fatigue quickly when riding, you may need a longer stem or even a frame with a longer top tube. If your lower back usually aches, the reach might be too long.

"The Europeans look down on raising your hands. They don't like the end-zone dance. I think that's unfortunate. That feeling— the finish line, the last couple of meters—is what motivates me."

—Lance Armstrong

Riding Buy Ways

The best time to get a great deal on a new bike is the end of summer (August and September). You can expect to save between 10 and 30 percent on models that have been sitting on the floor for a few months. Although you won't have the absolute latest gear, you're likely to get a great bike at a super price and the dealer is likely to give you an even better deal on shorts and summer clothing.

MONDAY

GOAL: ☐

ROUTE:

DISTANCE/TIME:

WEATHER CONDITIONS:

THOUGHTS:

TUESDAY

GOAL: ☐

ROUTE:

DISTANCE/TIME:

WEATHER CONDITIONS:

THOUGHTS:

WEDNESDAY

GOAL: ☐

ROUTE:

DISTANCE/TIME:

WEATHER CONDITIONS:

THOUGHTS:

THURSDAY

GOAL: ☐

ROUTE:

DISTANCE/TIME:

WEATHER CONDITIONS:

THOUGHTS:

FRIDAY

GOAL: ☐

ROUTE:

DISTANCE/TIME:

WEATHER CONDITIONS:

THOUGHTS:

SATURDAY

GOAL: ☐

ROUTE:

DISTANCE/TIME:

WEATHER CONDITIONS:

THOUGHTS:

SUNDAY

GOAL: ☐

ROUTE:

DISTANCE/TIME:

WEATHER CONDITIONS:

THOUGHTS:

WEEKLY TOTAL

TOTAL MILEAGE TO DATE

TIP OF THE WEEK

Float/No Float

Float refers to the amount of lateral heel movement that a clipless pedal system allows. If your old skateboarding injury is affecting your riding, you can get a system with lots of float. If you're an old pro and don't need any room to wiggle, get a system with zero float.

"I had to get 11 teeth replaced because I was grinding them. . . . It shows you how much pain I was in during the race. But the whole team in the Giro was supporting me [and] I didn't want to give up. I worked so hard to get to that point. It's amazing how you can put pain behind you."

—American cyclist Tyler Hamilton after placing second in the 2002 Tour of Italy

MONDAY

GOAL: ☐

ROUTE:

DISTANCE/TIME:

WEATHER CONDITIONS:

THOUGHTS:

TUESDAY

GOAL: ☐

ROUTE:

DISTANCE/TIME:

WEATHER CONDITIONS:

THOUGHTS:

WEDNESDAY

GOAL: ☐

ROUTE:

DISTANCE/TIME:

WEATHER CONDITIONS:

THOUGHTS:

THURSDAY

GOAL: ☐

ROUTE:

DISTANCE/TIME:

WEATHER CONDITIONS:

THOUGHTS:

FRIDAY

GOAL: ☐

ROUTE:

DISTANCE/TIME:

WEATHER CONDITIONS:

THOUGHTS:

SATURDAY

GOAL: ☐

ROUTE:

DISTANCE/TIME:

WEATHER CONDITIONS:

THOUGHTS:

SUNDAY

GOAL: ☐

ROUTE:

DISTANCE/TIME:

WEATHER CONDITIONS:

THOUGHTS:

WEEKLY TOTAL

TOTAL MILEAGE TO DATE

TIP OF THE WEEK

75/25 Sometimes

In a perfect world, about 75 percent of your stopping power comes from your front brake and 25 percent from the rear. That balance can change dramatically when conditions change. In wet or muddy conditions, use less of your front brake to avoid washing out the front wheel.

Keep Your Brakes Working

Clean your rims with soap and water and run a sheet of sandpaper over the brake pads on your road bike once every month. This will drastically improve braking by removing the fine layer of road grit and oil that builds up through regular use.

"Get a bicycle. You will certainly not regret it, if you live."

—*Mark Twain*

TIP OF THE WEEK

What's in That Goo?

One rule of thumb when deciding which energy gel is right for the ride you'll be doing is to look at the amount of sugar each serving contains. If a gel is high in sugar (8 or more grams per serving) then the easily digested sugars will fire you up for rides of 2 hours or less. If a gel is low in sugar or contains none at all, it's meant to be eaten on long, steady endurance rides.

MONDAY

GOAL:

ROUTE:

DISTANCE/TIME:

WEATHER CONDITIONS:

THOUGHTS:

TUESDAY

GOAL:

ROUTE:

DISTANCE/TIME:

WEATHER CONDITIONS:

THOUGHTS:

WEDNESDAY

GOAL:

ROUTE:

DISTANCE/TIME:

WEATHER CONDITIONS:

THOUGHTS:

THURSDAY

GOAL:

ROUTE:

DISTANCE/TIME:

WEATHER CONDITIONS:

THOUGHTS:

FRIDAY
GOAL: ☐

ROUTE:

DISTANCE/TIME:

WEATHER CONDITIONS:

THOUGHTS:

SATURDAY
GOAL: ☐

ROUTE:

DISTANCE/TIME:

WEATHER CONDITIONS:

THOUGHTS:

SUNDAY
GOAL: ☐

ROUTE:

DISTANCE/TIME:

WEATHER CONDITIONS:

THOUGHTS:

WEEKLY TOTAL

TOTAL MILEAGE TO DATE

Fend Off a Mountain Lion

Never turn and run. Instead, go face to face with the cat. Be sure to block your body with your bike and do anything to appear larger than you are: Spread your jacket wide, thrust your hands above your head, even lift your bike skyward. If attacked, use your bike to fend off the lion, aggressively swatting it in the head.

week of _____ to _____

"Never use your face as a brake pad."

—U.S. pro downhill mountain bike racer Jake Watson

Become a Better Climber

The best way to become a better climber is to lose weight. On a 3-mile climb with an average grade of 7 percent, a rider who weighs 170 pounds (including his bike and gear) will go a full minute faster than a rider weighing 180 pounds assuming that they're both putting out an average of 250 watts.

MONDAY

GOAL: ☐

ROUTE:

DISTANCE/TIME:

WEATHER CONDITIONS:

THOUGHTS:

TUESDAY

GOAL: ☐

ROUTE:

DISTANCE/TIME:

WEATHER CONDITIONS:

THOUGHTS:

WEDNESDAY

GOAL: ☐

ROUTE:

DISTANCE/TIME:

WEATHER CONDITIONS:

THOUGHTS:

THURSDAY

GOAL: ☐

ROUTE:

DISTANCE/TIME:

WEATHER CONDITIONS:

THOUGHTS:

FRIDAY

GOAL: ☐

ROUTE: _____

DISTANCE/TIME: _____

WEATHER CONDITIONS: _____

THOUGHTS: _____

SATURDAY

GOAL: ☐

ROUTE: _____

DISTANCE/TIME: _____

WEATHER CONDITIONS: _____

THOUGHTS: _____

SUNDAY

GOAL: ☐

ROUTE: _____

DISTANCE/TIME: _____

WEATHER CONDITIONS: _____

THOUGHTS: _____

WEEKLY TOTAL

_____

TOTAL MILEAGE TO DATE

_____

TIP OF THE WEEK

Comeback Kid

Has a traumatic crash kept you from getting back on your bike? You might recover faster if you set a goal—maybe a century or other organized ride—that's several months away and then start a slow buildup to the big day.

week of _____ to _____

"A pretty good diet I'd say."

—Graeme Obree, former hour record holder, regarding the diet of canned sardines, chili con carne, vegetables, and marmalade sandwiches that powered him through the "race of truth"

Survive a Front Flat Tire

Imagine that as you enter a corner your front tire blows out. A worst-case scenario for sure, but one you can survive if you have your wits together. As soon as the flat hits, stop leaning on the bike. Once you have it upright, you can apply the rear brake—under no circumstances should you hit the front brake. Once you have the bike slowed down, clip your foot out and, with your weight as far back as possible, put your foot on the ground. You've just survived a front flat.

MONDAY
GOAL: ☐

ROUTE:

DISTANCE/TIME:

WEATHER CONDITIONS:

THOUGHTS:

TUESDAY
GOAL: ☐

ROUTE:

DISTANCE/TIME:

WEATHER CONDITIONS:

THOUGHTS:

WEDNESDAY
GOAL: ☐

ROUTE:

DISTANCE/TIME:

WEATHER CONDITIONS:

THOUGHTS:

THURSDAY
GOAL: ☐

ROUTE:

DISTANCE/TIME:

WEATHER CONDITIONS:

THOUGHTS:

FRIDAY

GOAL: ☐

ROUTE:

DISTANCE/TIME:

WEATHER CONDITIONS:

THOUGHTS:

SATURDAY

GOAL: ☐

ROUTE:

DISTANCE/TIME:

WEATHER CONDITIONS:

THOUGHTS:

SUNDAY

GOAL: ☐

ROUTE:

DISTANCE/TIME:

WEATHER CONDITIONS:

THOUGHTS:

WEEKLY TOTAL

TOTAL MILEAGE TO DATE

TIP OF THE WEEK

Turn with Your Knees

On a fast descent, clamp your knees tight against the top tube. That'll keep the bike from vibrating at high speed and allow you to use small weight shifts to steer instead of turning the handlebars.

> **"Ours is certainly a very hard profession with terrible demands and painful sacrifices."**
>
> —Il Campionissimo Fausto Coppi regarding the life of a professional cyclist

Always Keep Your Bike Clean

After every ride spend 5 minutes doing the following and you'll rarely need to wash your bike:

1. Wipe down the frame, checking for dents or cracks as you go.
2. Lube the chain with a light lubricant.
3. Inspect the sidewall of each tire for cuts or tears.
4. Spin the wheels, making sure they are true.
5. Inspect the brake pads, making sure there is no less than 2 mm of usable pad. Any less and you've got to replace them.

MONDAY

GOAL: ☐

ROUTE:

DISTANCE/TIME:

WEATHER CONDITIONS:

THOUGHTS:

TUESDAY

GOAL: ☐

ROUTE:

DISTANCE/TIME:

WEATHER CONDITIONS:

THOUGHTS:

WEDNESDAY

GOAL: ☐

ROUTE:

DISTANCE/TIME:

WEATHER CONDITIONS:

THOUGHTS:

THURSDAY

GOAL: ☐

ROUTE:

DISTANCE/TIME:

WEATHER CONDITIONS:

THOUGHTS:

FRIDAY

GOAL: ☐

ROUTE:

DISTANCE/TIME:

WEATHER CONDITIONS:

THOUGHTS:

SATURDAY

GOAL: ☐

ROUTE:

DISTANCE/TIME:

WEATHER CONDITIONS:

THOUGHTS:

SUNDAY

GOAL: ☐

ROUTE:

DISTANCE/TIME:

WEATHER CONDITIONS:

THOUGHTS:

WEEKLY TOTAL

TOTAL MILEAGE TO DATE

TIP OF THE WEEK

Not Another Stroke?

If you're feeling so fatigued that you think you can't pedal another stroke, it may be the time to pedal harder. Drop one gear, and see if the change of cadence helps your legs recover. If that doesn't work, eat an energy bar or gel as soon as possible.

"I had learned what it means to ride the Tour de France. It's not about the bike. . . ."

—Lance Armstrong after winning a Tour de France stage in 1995, 2 days after the death of his teammate Fabio Casartelli on a high-speed descent

MONDAY

GOAL:

ROUTE:

DISTANCE/TIME:

WEATHER CONDITIONS:

THOUGHTS:

TUESDAY

GOAL:

ROUTE:

DISTANCE/TIME:

WEATHER CONDITIONS:

THOUGHTS:

Perfect Your Pedal Stroke

This winter, if you spend as little as an hour a week riding rollers, your pedal stroke will be picture-perfect next spring. Unlike resistance trainers, free-standing rollers reward a smooth, supple pedal stroke because they force you to balance your bike. If you're truly determined to refine your spin, put together a fixed gear bike (one gear, no coasting) with brakes. It'll be perfect for roller riding and can be used for training rides focused on improving your pedaling technique.

WEDNESDAY

GOAL:

ROUTE:

DISTANCE/TIME:

WEATHER CONDITIONS:

THOUGHTS:

THURSDAY

GOAL:

ROUTE:

DISTANCE/TIME:

WEATHER CONDITIONS:

THOUGHTS:

FRIDAY

GOAL: ☐

ROUTE:

DISTANCE/TIME:

WEATHER CONDITIONS:

THOUGHTS:

SATURDAY

GOAL: ☐

ROUTE:

DISTANCE/TIME:

WEATHER CONDITIONS:

THOUGHTS:

SUNDAY

GOAL: ☐

ROUTE:

DISTANCE/TIME:

WEATHER CONDITIONS:

THOUGHTS:

WEEKLY TOTAL

TOTAL MILEAGE TO DATE

TIP OF THE WEEK

Zero In

Having trouble getting your bike to go exactly where you want it to on the trail? Try the following: Look about 10 feet down the trail and zero in on exactly where you want your front tire to go—not the millions of places you don't want it to go. This will help you nail just the right line every time.

> "Cycle tracks
> will abound in
> Utopia."

—*H. G. Wells*

Do Just the Right Amount of Work

When riding with a group, you should never do more than your share of the work, but then again, you shouldn't do too little either. Keep in mind that it's not your responsibility to get the group to the finish and do the minimum amount of work that maintains the group's speed. When you take a pull on the front of the group, your aim should be to keep the pace of the rider who pulled through before you.

MONDAY
GOAL: ☐

ROUTE:

DISTANCE/TIME:

WEATHER CONDITIONS:

THOUGHTS:

TUESDAY
GOAL: ☐

ROUTE:

DISTANCE/TIME:

WEATHER CONDITIONS:

THOUGHTS:

WEDNESDAY
GOAL: ☐

ROUTE:

DISTANCE/TIME:

WEATHER CONDITIONS:

THOUGHTS:

THURSDAY
GOAL: ☐

ROUTE:

DISTANCE/TIME:

WEATHER CONDITIONS:

THOUGHTS:

FRIDAY

GOAL: ☐

ROUTE:

DISTANCE/TIME:

WEATHER CONDITIONS:

THOUGHTS:

SATURDAY

GOAL: ☐

ROUTE:

DISTANCE/TIME:

WEATHER CONDITIONS:

THOUGHTS:

SUNDAY

GOAL: ☐

ROUTE:

DISTANCE/TIME:

WEATHER CONDITIONS:

THOUGHTS:

TIP OF THE WEEK

Height Right?

Think you've got your saddle height right? Even the great Eddy Merckx was constantly changing his seat position, sometimes midrace! That's a little extreme, but you can use the off-season to experiment with your height and fore-and-aft adjustment. Make changes in ultra-small increments.

WEEKLY TOTAL

TOTAL MILEAGE TO DATE

"Think of bicycles as ridable art that can just about save the world."

—Grant Petersen, founder and owner of Rivendell Cycles

Treat a Saddle Sore

A saddle sore is either an area of chafing or a small, pimply looking bacterial infection anywhere your shorts hit you. If you keep riding on one without proper treatment, it can turn into a major infection that could require surgery. The best treatment is a couple days without riding and an over-the-counter antibiotic ointment such as Polysporin. If you're in the middle of an extended bike trip and can't sit out a day, apply some type of second skin, such as moleskin, to reduce pressure and friction. Be sure to cut a doughnut-shaped patch large enough to fit around the affected area.

MONDAY

GOAL: ☐

ROUTE:

DISTANCE/TIME:

WEATHER CONDITIONS:

THOUGHTS:

TUESDAY

GOAL: ☐

ROUTE:

DISTANCE/TIME:

WEATHER CONDITIONS:

THOUGHTS:

WEDNESDAY

GOAL: ☐

ROUTE:

DISTANCE/TIME:

WEATHER CONDITIONS:

THOUGHTS:

THURSDAY

GOAL: ☐

ROUTE:

DISTANCE/TIME:

WEATHER CONDITIONS:

THOUGHTS:

FRIDAY

GOAL: ☐

ROUTE:

DISTANCE/TIME:

WEATHER CONDITIONS:

THOUGHTS:

SATURDAY

GOAL: ☐

ROUTE:

DISTANCE/TIME:

WEATHER CONDITIONS:

THOUGHTS:

SUNDAY

GOAL: ☐

ROUTE:

DISTANCE/TIME:

WEATHER CONDITIONS:

THOUGHTS:

WEEKLY TOTAL

TOTAL MILEAGE TO DATE

TIP OF THE WEEK

60-Minute Rule

You should be eating your preride/prerace meal about 2 hours before you're due to start. If there's less than an hour to go, skip the meal entirely. Eat a few energy bars that you know sit well in your system, and eat more than normal during the event (once every 20 minutes should do it).

"I don't talk unless I'm winning. If I'm not winning, you won't hear a word from me. But I like to win, and when I win, I'm a big mouth. That's just the way I am."

—*Mountain bike, ski, and snowboard champion Shaun Palmer*

Sore Excuses

To reduce your risk of getting saddle sores, try these three steps:
1. Stay clean. Keep your shorts and your body as clean as possible and don't wear shorts more than once without washing.
2. Soften the pad in your shorts by rubbing A&D Ointment with zinc oxide on your pad and your skin if necessary.
3. Once you've settled on a saddle that's comfortable for you, be sure to set it up properly on your bike.

MONDAY

GOAL: ☐

ROUTE:

DISTANCE/TIME:

WEATHER CONDITIONS:

THOUGHTS:

TUESDAY

GOAL: ☐

ROUTE:

DISTANCE/TIME:

WEATHER CONDITIONS:

THOUGHTS:

WEDNESDAY

GOAL: ☐

ROUTE:

DISTANCE/TIME:

WEATHER CONDITIONS:

THOUGHTS:

THURSDAY

GOAL: ☐

ROUTE:

DISTANCE/TIME:

WEATHER CONDITIONS:

THOUGHTS:

FRIDAY

GOAL: ☐

ROUTE:

DISTANCE/TIME:

WEATHER CONDITIONS:

THOUGHTS:

SATURDAY

GOAL: ☐

ROUTE:

DISTANCE/TIME:

WEATHER CONDITIONS:

THOUGHTS:

SUNDAY

GOAL: ☐

ROUTE:

DISTANCE/TIME:

WEATHER CONDITIONS:

THOUGHTS:

TIP OF THE WEEK

Rollin' thru Ronald's

Need a quick, hot bite before a race? Pull into the drive-thru at McDonald's and order an Egg McMuffin. It's got just 300 calories, 18 grams of protein, 29 grams of carbs, and 12 grams of fat. Not bad for a buck.

WEEKLY TOTAL

TOTAL MILEAGE TO DATE

"You get a feeling on certain trails, when you're reacting like you and your machine are just one thing. It's the feeling of physical exertion and speed and technique all wrapped into one."

—*American Ned Overend, winner of the first-ever UCI mountain bike world championships*

TIP OF THE WEEK

Just like Running

Steep out-of-the-saddle climbs are hell on sloppy pedalers. To get smoother strokes, pull your leg up and wrap it over the top of the stroke. Imagine you're running over 2-foot-high barriers, bringing your leg up and around for each big step.

MONDAY
GOAL: ☐
ROUTE:
DISTANCE/TIME:
WEATHER CONDITIONS:
THOUGHTS:

TUESDAY
GOAL: ☐
ROUTE:
DISTANCE/TIME:
WEATHER CONDITIONS:
THOUGHTS:

WEDNESDAY
GOAL: ☐
ROUTE:
DISTANCE/TIME:
WEATHER CONDITIONS:
THOUGHTS:

THURSDAY
GOAL: ☐
ROUTE:
DISTANCE/TIME:
WEATHER CONDITIONS:
THOUGHTS:

FRIDAY

GOAL: ☐

ROUTE:

DISTANCE/TIME:

WEATHER CONDITIONS:

THOUGHTS:

SATURDAY

GOAL: ☐

ROUTE:

DISTANCE/TIME:

WEATHER CONDITIONS:

THOUGHTS:

SUNDAY

GOAL: ☐

ROUTE:

DISTANCE/TIME:

WEATHER CONDITIONS:

THOUGHTS:

WEEKLY TOTAL

TOTAL MILEAGE TO DATE

Use a Heart Rate Monitor

Once you know your maximum heart rate (you can determine this through a VO_2 max test or by informal field testing), you can reliably base all of your training on that number. Here's how:

- 50 to 70 percent of maximum is the zone where you're building endurance energy systems and actively promoting recovery from your more difficult rides.
- 70 to 80 percent of maximum is the zone where you'll build your aerobic muscular endurance and refine the systems that provide energy for your muscles when under stress.
- 80 to 90 percent is the zone where you cross over your anaerobic or lactate threshold. Training just above and below this threshold is the best way to improve your high-end fitness.
- 95 to 100 percent of your maximum is the zone where you're overtaxing your muscles so dramatically that it is reserved for peak training efforts at your peak of fitness. Many people never train at this level.

"He's won the Tour so many times and I really don't think I can even win the Tour de France."

—*Lance Armstrong in 1987 when asked how he thought about being "the next Greg LeMond"*

Get Faster Quick

Once you have a good base of aerobic fitness—at least 2 solid months' worth—you can boost your speed quickly by doing short, high-intensity intervals. Over-geared jumps give you faster acceleration and more muscle power in the saddle. From a cruising speed of 15 to 20 mph in a hard gear such as 53x12- 15-tooth, stomp on the pedals for 15 to 20 seconds while staying in the saddle. Do 1 or 2 sets of 3 to 5 intervals with a full recovery between efforts and a 10-minute recovery between sets. These intervals can be integrated into any ride that you'd normally do.

MONDAY
GOAL: ☐
ROUTE:
DISTANCE/TIME:
WEATHER CONDITIONS:
THOUGHTS:

TUESDAY
GOAL: ☐
ROUTE:
DISTANCE/TIME:
WEATHER CONDITIONS:
THOUGHTS:

WEDNESDAY
GOAL: ☐
ROUTE:
DISTANCE/TIME:
WEATHER CONDITIONS:
THOUGHTS:

THURSDAY
GOAL: ☐
ROUTE:
DISTANCE/TIME:
WEATHER CONDITIONS:
THOUGHTS:

FRIDAY

GOAL: ☐

ROUTE:

DISTANCE/TIME:

WEATHER CONDITIONS:

THOUGHTS:

SATURDAY

GOAL: ☐

ROUTE:

DISTANCE/TIME:

WEATHER CONDITIONS:

THOUGHTS:

SUNDAY

GOAL: ☐

ROUTE:

DISTANCE/TIME:

WEATHER CONDITIONS:

THOUGHTS:

WEEKLY TOTAL

TOTAL MILEAGE TO DATE

TIP OF THE WEEK

Have a Drink

Recovery drinks such as Endurox R4 are the ideal way to refuel after a tough ride because they hydrate you and give you the correct 4:1 mix of carbs to protein. Yet you can also get the right mix with regular foods such as a bean and vegetable burrito or a triple-layer turkey sandwich.

"The truly extraordinary feature of the bike is that, like the greatest teacher, it encourages you to find the answers from somewhere deep down inside yourself. . . ."

—*author Tom Davies*

Be Rested but Ready

Of course you don't want to train hard right before a big ride or race, but if you're going to take a day off, do it 2 days prior to the event. Against all logic, an easy day can leave you rested but sluggish the following day. Instead, on the day before the event, go for a 2-hour ride with a few short, high-intensity bursts. This will test your body and give it a preview of what's to come.

MONDAY

GOAL: ☐

ROUTE:

DISTANCE/TIME:

WEATHER CONDITIONS:

THOUGHTS:

TUESDAY

GOAL: ☐

ROUTE:

DISTANCE/TIME:

WEATHER CONDITIONS:

THOUGHTS:

WEDNESDAY

GOAL: ☐

ROUTE:

DISTANCE/TIME:

WEATHER CONDITIONS:

THOUGHTS:

THURSDAY

GOAL: ☐

ROUTE:

DISTANCE/TIME:

WEATHER CONDITIONS:

THOUGHTS:

FRIDAY

GOAL: ☐

ROUTE:

DISTANCE/TIME:

WEATHER CONDITIONS:

THOUGHTS:

SATURDAY

GOAL: ☐

ROUTE:

DISTANCE/TIME:

WEATHER CONDITIONS:

THOUGHTS:

SUNDAY

GOAL: ☐

ROUTE:

DISTANCE/TIME:

WEATHER CONDITIONS:

THOUGHTS:

TIP OF THE WEEK

Hit the Window

Having trouble riding hard on consecutive days? You may not be eating at the right time. Studies have shown that inhaling food within 30 minutes after a ride, when your "glycogen window" is open, allows your body to convert carbohydrates into stored energy at a super-efficient pace. For best results eat a 4:1 ratio of carbs to proteins.

WEEKLY TOTAL

TOTAL MILEAGE TO DATE

"The more I think about our U.S. domestic transportation problems, the more I see an increased role for the bicycle in American life."

—*George H. W. Bush during his tenure as ambassador to China*

Avoid Being Dropped on a Climb

Even if climbing isn't your strong point, there's no reason you can't keep from getting dropped. If you know there's a climb coming, be sure that you're in the front of the group if not slightly ahead of it. As you gradually drift back during the toughest portions of the climb, you'll be able to pace off riders who would normally be in front of you. Time it correctly, and you'll just be hitting the back of the group as you make the top of the climb.

MONDAY
GOAL: ☐
ROUTE:
DISTANCE/TIME:
WEATHER CONDITIONS:
THOUGHTS:

TUESDAY
GOAL: ☐
ROUTE:
DISTANCE/TIME:
WEATHER CONDITIONS:
THOUGHTS:

WEDNESDAY
GOAL: ☐
ROUTE:
DISTANCE/TIME:
WEATHER CONDITIONS:
THOUGHTS:

THURSDAY
GOAL: ☐
ROUTE:
DISTANCE/TIME:
WEATHER CONDITIONS:
THOUGHTS:

FRIDAY

GOAL: ☐

ROUTE:

DISTANCE/TIME:

WEATHER CONDITIONS:

THOUGHTS:

SATURDAY

GOAL: ☐

ROUTE:

DISTANCE/TIME:

WEATHER CONDITIONS:

THOUGHTS:

SUNDAY

GOAL: ☐

ROUTE:

DISTANCE/TIME:

WEATHER CONDITIONS:

THOUGHTS:

WEEKLY TOTAL

TOTAL MILEAGE TO DATE

TIP OF THE WEEK

Outsmart Altitude

You can't acclimate to high altitude in a weekend—studies show that it takes most people about 3 weeks—but you can make the best of the thin air by staying hydrated, protecting yourself from intense UV rays that often grow stronger as you move closer to the sun, and by resting as much as possible. On the bike you'll want to stay well below your maximum effort. Once you overcook it at altitude, you'll have an incredibly difficult time coming back.

> "The most important factor you can keep in your own hands is yourself. I always placed the greatest emphasis on that."
>
> —*Eddy Merckx*

Recover from an Incredibly Hard Ride

You're just finishing a hard day on the bike, awash in an endorphin glow, but dreading the way you'll feel tomorrow. Here's a great strategy for maximum recovery.

When you finish riding, consume 50 to 100 grams of carbohydrates and 15 to 30 grams of protein within a half hour. For example, have a turkey or peanut butter sandwich on wheat or spelt bread and 12 to 16 ounces of recovery drink with a balance of one protein for every four carbs. After you've done that, continue to drink as much water as you can.

MONDAY
GOAL: ☐
ROUTE:
DISTANCE/TIME:
WEATHER CONDITIONS:
THOUGHTS:

TUESDAY
GOAL: ☐
ROUTE:
DISTANCE/TIME:
WEATHER CONDITIONS:
THOUGHTS:

WEDNESDAY
GOAL: ☐
ROUTE:
DISTANCE/TIME:
WEATHER CONDITIONS:
THOUGHTS:

THURSDAY
GOAL: ☐
ROUTE:
DISTANCE/TIME:
WEATHER CONDITIONS:
THOUGHTS:

FRIDAY

GOAL: ☐

ROUTE:

DISTANCE/TIME:

WEATHER CONDITIONS:

THOUGHTS:

SATURDAY

GOAL: ☐

ROUTE:

DISTANCE/TIME:

WEATHER CONDITIONS:

THOUGHTS:

SUNDAY

GOAL: ☐

ROUTE:

DISTANCE/TIME:

WEATHER CONDITIONS:

THOUGHTS:

WEEKLY TOTAL

TOTAL MILEAGE TO DATE

TIP OF THE WEEK

The Special

One of the best foods to eat on the morning of a big ride or race is a three-egg spinach omelet with a side of whole-grain toast. The omelet will stay with you long into the ride and, because it's not packed with sugar like pancakes, waffles or most breakfast cereals, you won't bonk. Try to avoid cheese in the omelet and jam on the toast—they're extras that a well-prepared body doesn't need on race day.

> "When I see an adult on a bicycle, I do not despair for the future of the human race."

—H. G. Wells

Always Train with a Purpose

Most riders spend too much time training. If you focus your riding based on the type of event(s) that you're working for, you can highly specify your training and reduce the amount of hours you spend in the saddle. If you're doing a mountain bike race that's under 2 hours, there's no reason to train for longer than 2 hours. In fact, you should focus all of your training between 1 and 2 hours, working the anaerobic systems that fuel your most intense efforts.

MONDAY
GOAL: ☐

ROUTE:

DISTANCE/TIME:

WEATHER CONDITIONS:

THOUGHTS:

TUESDAY
GOAL: ☐

ROUTE:

DISTANCE/TIME:

WEATHER CONDITIONS:

THOUGHTS:

WEDNESDAY
GOAL: ☐

ROUTE:

DISTANCE/TIME:

WEATHER CONDITIONS:

THOUGHTS:

THURSDAY
GOAL: ☐

ROUTE:

DISTANCE/TIME:

WEATHER CONDITIONS:

THOUGHTS:

FRIDAY
GOAL: ☐

ROUTE:

DISTANCE/TIME:

WEATHER CONDITIONS:

THOUGHTS:

SATURDAY
GOAL: ☐

ROUTE:

DISTANCE/TIME:

WEATHER CONDITIONS:

THOUGHTS:

SUNDAY
GOAL: ☐

ROUTE:

DISTANCE/TIME:

WEATHER CONDITIONS:

THOUGHTS:

TIP OF THE WEEK

Go Nuts!

Peanuts have a bad rep for high fat content (26 grams per 1.75-ounce pack of dry-roasted nuts). But the monounsaturated oils in peanuts have nearly the same cholesterol-lowering effects as olive oil and may help you "go nuts" on a bike.

WEEKLY TOTAL

TOTAL MILEAGE TO DATE

"Another great superiority of the bicycle lies in the fact that you can always get rid of it when you wish. You can roll it in and stand it up in a corner and there it stays."

—*a late-19th-century article in the* Minneapolis Tribune

Keep Riding Fun

Even when preparing for a big event, your riding should be fun. If you hit a tough patch in your training, take a day or two off and tune up your bike. Or, better yet, go for a fun ride with your kids or burn some energy doing errands around town. You'll be surprised how much more focused and intense your training will be after the break.

MONDAY

GOAL: ☐

ROUTE:

DISTANCE/TIME:

WEATHER CONDITIONS:

THOUGHTS:

TUESDAY

GOAL: ☐

ROUTE:

DISTANCE/TIME:

WEATHER CONDITIONS:

THOUGHTS:

WEDNESDAY

GOAL: ☐

ROUTE:

DISTANCE/TIME:

WEATHER CONDITIONS:

THOUGHTS:

THURSDAY

GOAL: ☐

ROUTE:

DISTANCE/TIME:

WEATHER CONDITIONS:

THOUGHTS:

FRIDAY

GOAL: ☐

ROUTE:

DISTANCE/TIME:

WEATHER CONDITIONS:

THOUGHTS:

SATURDAY

GOAL: ☐

ROUTE:

DISTANCE/TIME:

WEATHER CONDITIONS:

THOUGHTS:

SUNDAY

GOAL: ☐

ROUTE:

DISTANCE/TIME:

WEATHER CONDITIONS:

THOUGHTS:

WEEKLY TOTAL

TOTAL MILEAGE TO DATE

TIP OF THE WEEK

Walk It Off

At the end of a brutally difficult ride or race, don't collapse; instead, cool down. If you stop dead at the end of a ride, blood will pool in your extremities. That can leave you feeling light-headed, and you're more likely to feel soreness in your muscles the following day. Just 20 minutes of easy spinning or even walking will clean the blood and lactic acid from your legs and leave you feeling fresh the following day.

"**When in doubt, gas it!**"

—*Greg Herbold,*
U.S. pro downhill
mountain bike racer

Never Forget Anything

The sure way to never forget anything when you're packing for a ride or a race is to have a mental checklist. Start with your helmet and work your way down—sunglasses, jacket, jersey, undershirt, shorts, socks, shoes. Then go over your bike from the top down—pump, spare tube, water bottles, energy food. Whatever order you use, always keep it the same and you'll be unlikely to forget even the smallest detail.

MONDAY
GOAL: ☐

ROUTE:

DISTANCE/TIME:

WEATHER CONDITIONS:

THOUGHTS:

TUESDAY
GOAL: ☐

ROUTE:

DISTANCE/TIME:

WEATHER CONDITIONS:

THOUGHTS:

WEDNESDAY
GOAL: ☐

ROUTE:

DISTANCE/TIME:

WEATHER CONDITIONS:

THOUGHTS:

THURSDAY
GOAL: ☐

ROUTE:

DISTANCE/TIME:

WEATHER CONDITIONS:

THOUGHTS:

FRIDAY

GOAL: ☐

ROUTE: _____

DISTANCE/TIME: _____

WEATHER CONDITIONS: _____

THOUGHTS: _____

SATURDAY

GOAL: ☐

ROUTE: _____

DISTANCE/TIME: _____

WEATHER CONDITIONS: _____

THOUGHTS: _____

SUNDAY

GOAL: ☐

ROUTE: _____

DISTANCE/TIME: _____

WEATHER CONDITIONS: _____

THOUGHTS: _____

_____

WEEKLY TOTAL

_____

TOTAL MILEAGE TO DATE

_____

TIP OF THE WEEK

Newtons Still Rule

In an unfamiliar place and can't find an energy bar? Head to the grocery store's cookie aisle and grab some Fig Newtons. Each Fig Newton is packed with 22 grams of carbs, a gram of fiber, and plenty of potassium, iron, and calcium. Just three to four Fig Newtons contain the same caloric content as a typical energy bar.

week of _____ to _____

"Until you put yourself to the test, there's always fear. My test is whether I can still leave the others behind on a climb like I used to before."

—*Tour de France and Tour of Italy winner Marco Pantani*

Get Your Bike on a Plane for Free

The most truthful way to avoid the fee that airlines charge for bikes is to have a folding bike or a full-sized "travel" bike equipped with S&S Couplings. That will allow you to fit the bike into a 26×26×10-inch case that is well within normal baggage size. You'll have to shell out at least $500 extra for an S&S frame and hard case, but you can recoup that amount in just five round-trip flights.

MONDAY

GOAL:

ROUTE:

DISTANCE/TIME:

WEATHER CONDITIONS:

THOUGHTS:

TUESDAY

GOAL:

ROUTE:

DISTANCE/TIME:

WEATHER CONDITIONS:

THOUGHTS:

WEDNESDAY

GOAL:

ROUTE:

DISTANCE/TIME:

WEATHER CONDITIONS:

THOUGHTS:

THURSDAY

GOAL:

ROUTE:

DISTANCE/TIME:

WEATHER CONDITIONS:

THOUGHTS:

FRIDAY

GOAL: ☐

ROUTE: _____

DISTANCE/TIME: _____

WEATHER CONDITIONS: _____

THOUGHTS: _____

SATURDAY

GOAL: ☐

ROUTE: _____

DISTANCE/TIME: _____

WEATHER CONDITIONS: _____

THOUGHTS: _____

SUNDAY

GOAL: ☐

ROUTE: _____

DISTANCE/TIME: _____

WEATHER CONDITIONS: _____

THOUGHTS: _____

TIP OF THE WEEK

Climb like Lance?

He's known for exhausting his rivals with a high cadence on climbs, but his secret for increasing brute climbing strength and power is muscle tension intervals. Armstrong's known to climb a steady grade at a low 60 rpm for 15 minutes. He recovers and then does it three more times for a complete session.

WEEKLY TOTAL

_____

TOTAL MILEAGE TO DATE

_____

"If you don't accept victory graciously, you may not be able to do the same in defeat."

—five-time Tour de France winner Miguel Indurain

Get a Racing License and Find a Race

Most road, track, and mountain bike races in the United States require a United States Cycling Federation (USCF) or a National Off-Road Bicycling Association (NORBA) racing license that costs $50 for an annual license or just $5 for a 1-day beginner license. To find a race, log on to the USA Cycling Web site (www.usacycling.org). It lists individual events and clubs that host events in your area.

MONDAY

GOAL: ☐

ROUTE:

DISTANCE/TIME:

WEATHER CONDITIONS:

THOUGHTS:

TUESDAY

GOAL: ☐

ROUTE:

DISTANCE/TIME:

WEATHER CONDITIONS:

THOUGHTS:

WEDNESDAY

GOAL: ☐

ROUTE:

DISTANCE/TIME:

WEATHER CONDITIONS:

THOUGHTS:

THURSDAY

GOAL: ☐

ROUTE:

DISTANCE/TIME:

WEATHER CONDITIONS:

THOUGHTS:

FRIDAY

GOAL: ☐

ROUTE:

DISTANCE/TIME:

WEATHER CONDITIONS:

THOUGHTS:

SATURDAY

GOAL: ☐

ROUTE:

DISTANCE/TIME:

WEATHER CONDITIONS:

THOUGHTS:

SUNDAY

GOAL: ☐

ROUTE:

DISTANCE/TIME:

WEATHER CONDITIONS:

THOUGHTS:

TIP OF THE WEEK

Beat the Bonk

You can ensure that you won't bonk midride by following a simple 20-minute rule. Starting 40 minutes after the start of your ride, eat something every 20 minutes. It can be just a bite or two of energy bar or an entire packet of gel, but if you eat on schedule you'll never run out of energy.

WEEKLY TOTAL

TOTAL MILEAGE TO DATE

week of _____ to _____

"I'm exhausted and overjoyed."

—*Tour de France winner Jan Ullrich in the midst of his battle with Lance Armstrong during the 2003 Tour. He went on to finish second.*

Ride with Lance Armstrong

You idolize Lance Armstrong and would give your left leg to ride with the cancer survivor and Tour champion. For most of us, the only sure way to clinch a ride with Lance is to become one of the top fundraisers in the Lance Armstrong Foundation's Peloton Project. Every fall at Armstrong's Ride for the Roses fundraising weekend, the Peloton Project members that have raised the most cash get to go for a spin with Lance. Go to www.laf.org for more information.

MONDAY
GOAL: ☐

ROUTE: _____

DISTANCE/TIME: _____

WEATHER CONDITIONS: _____

THOUGHTS: _____

TUESDAY
GOAL: ☐

ROUTE: _____

DISTANCE/TIME: _____

WEATHER CONDITIONS: _____

THOUGHTS: _____

WEDNESDAY
GOAL: ☐

ROUTE: _____

DISTANCE/TIME: _____

WEATHER CONDITIONS: _____

THOUGHTS: _____

THURSDAY
GOAL: ☐

ROUTE: _____

DISTANCE/TIME: _____

WEATHER CONDITIONS: _____

THOUGHTS: _____

FRIDAY

GOAL: ☐

ROUTE:

DISTANCE/TIME:

WEATHER CONDITIONS:

THOUGHTS:

SATURDAY

GOAL: ☐

ROUTE:

DISTANCE/TIME:

WEATHER CONDITIONS:

THOUGHTS:

SUNDAY

GOAL: ☐

ROUTE:

DISTANCE/TIME:

WEATHER CONDITIONS:

THOUGHTS:

WEEKLY TOTAL

TOTAL MILEAGE TO DATE

TIP OF THE WEEK

Hydrate, Hydrate, Hydrate

If you know you've got a ride or event that's likely to take place on a hot day, train your body to hold more water than it normally would by hydrating consistently in the days just before the ride. That way you won't start the event with low-grade dehydration. In the hours just prior to the start, be sure that you're constantly drinking water and avoid caffeinated drinks like coffee and soda.

"It is by riding a bicycle that you learn the contours of a country best, since you have to sweat up the hills and coast down them."

—Ernest Hemingway

Ice an Injury

The best way to minimize the damage caused from an impact injury like a fall or a collision with another rider is to apply ice to the damaged area as soon as possible.

Using cubes of ice in a plastic bag, apply directly to the injured area. Do not ice for longer than 15 minutes at a time, as you could cause nerve damage or even frostbite to the affected area. Once the affected area is warm to the touch, you can apply ice again. Repeat as often as necessary.

MONDAY

GOAL: ☐

ROUTE:

DISTANCE/TIME:

WEATHER CONDITIONS:

THOUGHTS:

TUESDAY

GOAL: ☐

ROUTE:

DISTANCE/TIME:

WEATHER CONDITIONS:

THOUGHTS:

WEDNESDAY

GOAL: ☐

ROUTE:

DISTANCE/TIME:

WEATHER CONDITIONS:

THOUGHTS:

THURSDAY

GOAL: ☐

ROUTE:

DISTANCE/TIME:

WEATHER CONDITIONS:

THOUGHTS:

FRIDAY

GOAL: ☐

ROUTE:

DISTANCE/TIME:

WEATHER CONDITIONS:

THOUGHTS:

SATURDAY

GOAL: ☐

ROUTE:

DISTANCE/TIME:

WEATHER CONDITIONS:

THOUGHTS:

SUNDAY

GOAL: ☐

ROUTE:

DISTANCE/TIME:

WEATHER CONDITIONS:

THOUGHTS:

WEEKLY TOTAL

TOTAL MILEAGE TO DATE

TIP OF THE WEEK

Who's the Boss?

Is there a brutal hill on your favorite ride? Don't dread or simply suffer through it; kick its butt. Set a tempo that you can hold the entire length of the climb and search for familiar landmarks—a sign post, a mailbox, a tree, et cetera. As you climb, power past each one. When you near the summit, shift down, get out of the saddle, and power over the top.

> "What makes a great endurance athlete is the ability to absorb potential embarrassment, and to suffer without complaint."
>
> —Lance Armstrong

MONDAY

GOAL: ☐

ROUTE:

DISTANCE/TIME:

WEATHER CONDITIONS:

THOUGHTS:

TUESDAY

GOAL: ☐

ROUTE:

DISTANCE/TIME:

WEATHER CONDITIONS:

THOUGHTS:

Ride Easy

Whether you're on a structured training program or simply riding when you can, you should spend a certain number of days riding easy. It could be a simple spin in the days before a big event or a day of active recovery from that big ride. To make sure your body recovers, keep your heart rate at 40 to 60 percent of its maximum. You should be riding easily enough that you can have a conversation with a friend or sing a song without gasping for air.

WEDNESDAY

GOAL: ☐

ROUTE:

DISTANCE/TIME:

WEATHER CONDITIONS:

THOUGHTS:

THURSDAY

GOAL: ☐

ROUTE:

DISTANCE/TIME:

WEATHER CONDITIONS:

THOUGHTS:

FRIDAY

GOAL: ☐

ROUTE:

DISTANCE/TIME:

WEATHER CONDITIONS:

THOUGHTS:

SATURDAY

GOAL: ☐

ROUTE:

DISTANCE/TIME:

WEATHER CONDITIONS:

THOUGHTS:

SUNDAY

GOAL: ☐

ROUTE:

DISTANCE/TIME:

WEATHER CONDITIONS:

THOUGHTS:

WEEKLY TOTAL

TOTAL MILEAGE TO DATE

TIP OF THE WEEK

Cut the Caffeine

Trade your morning joe for a cup of green tea. "The caffeine in coffee depletes your adrenal glands, and hard riding is already a stress on the adrenals," says Lydia Faesy, a naturopathic physician who treats endurance athletes. Green tea has 20 percent of the caffeine in coffee, and it's full of beneficial antioxidants, which help your body repair and prevent muscle damage.

"I worked myself to the bone. Now, looking back, I realize I was made to do so."

—*Eddy Merckx*

Keep Trails Open

Trail access is an issue that, with increasing user numbers and a more finely tuned environmental sensitivity, will never die down. The best way to ensure the trails you love remain open for everyone is to join the world's leading trail advocacy group, the International Mountain Bike Association (www.IMBA.com). IMBA creates, enhances, and preserves trails and access to them for all user groups. Individual memberships start at just $25—less than the entrance fee at an amusement park.

MONDAY

GOAL:

ROUTE:

DISTANCE/TIME:

WEATHER CONDITIONS:

THOUGHTS:

TUESDAY

GOAL:

ROUTE:

DISTANCE/TIME:

WEATHER CONDITIONS:

THOUGHTS:

WEDNESDAY

GOAL:

ROUTE:

DISTANCE/TIME:

WEATHER CONDITIONS:

THOUGHTS:

THURSDAY

GOAL:

ROUTE:

DISTANCE/TIME:

WEATHER CONDITIONS:

THOUGHTS:

FRIDAY
GOAL: ☐

ROUTE:

DISTANCE/TIME:

WEATHER CONDITIONS:

THOUGHTS:

SATURDAY
GOAL: ☐

ROUTE:

DISTANCE/TIME:

WEATHER CONDITIONS:

THOUGHTS:

SUNDAY
GOAL: ☐

ROUTE:

DISTANCE/TIME:

WEATHER CONDITIONS:

THOUGHTS:

WEEKLY TOTAL

TOTAL MILEAGE TO DATE

TIP OF THE WEEK

Libido Limp?

Has your interest in sex fallen right off the back of the back of the pack? If your libido is not what you think it should be, you might be training too hard. Take a couple of days or a long weekend off the bike, and spend that time with your partner. Soon enough you'll be back in action and your home life will be better than ever.

"Most of cycling is not the Tour de France. It's not glamorous. And a lot of it is just plain hard, ugly, and miserable."

—*Greg LeMond*

Make Your Shorts Last Longer

Until the last decade the best cycling shorts used real chamois pads. When properly cared for they were incredibly comfortable, but keeping them soft and pliant was a pain in the ... well, you get it. Today's shorts are easier to care for but will stay most comfortable and last longest if you follow the old-school rules for care. Always hand-wash using Woolite or some other specially formulated detergent. Always hang them to dry; mechanical dryers will make the pad stiff and ruin the Lycra. Rub an antibacterial ointment or salve into the pad to ensure cleanliness and maximum suppleness.

MONDAY
GOAL:
ROUTE:
DISTANCE/TIME:
WEATHER CONDITIONS:
THOUGHTS:

TUESDAY
GOAL:
ROUTE:
DISTANCE/TIME:
WEATHER CONDITIONS:
THOUGHTS:

WEDNESDAY
GOAL:
ROUTE:
DISTANCE/TIME:
WEATHER CONDITIONS:
THOUGHTS:

THURSDAY
GOAL:
ROUTE:
DISTANCE/TIME:
WEATHER CONDITIONS:
THOUGHTS:

FRIDAY

GOAL: ☐

ROUTE:

DISTANCE/TIME:

WEATHER CONDITIONS:

THOUGHTS:

SATURDAY

GOAL: ☐

ROUTE:

DISTANCE/TIME:

WEATHER CONDITIONS:

THOUGHTS:

SUNDAY

GOAL: ☐

ROUTE:

DISTANCE/TIME:

WEATHER CONDITIONS:

THOUGHTS:

WEEKLY TOTAL

TOTAL MILEAGE TO DATE

TIP OF THE WEEK

Good Fat

Be sure to include fatty fish (especially salmon) in your diet. The polyunsaturated omega-3 fat will lower the triglyceride and cholesterol levels in your body, boost your immune system, give your skin a healthy glow, and ensure proper nerve function. Try two servings a week.

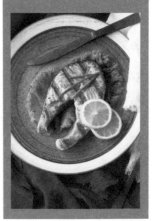

"Bicycling is a big part of the future. It has to be. There is something wrong with a society that drives a car to work out in a gym."

—Bill Nye, scientist and producer of public TV science programs

MONDAY
GOAL: ☐
ROUTE:
DISTANCE/TIME:
WEATHER CONDITIONS:
THOUGHTS:

TUESDAY
GOAL: ☐
ROUTE:
DISTANCE/TIME:
WEATHER CONDITIONS:
THOUGHTS:

Never Bonk on a Long Ride

To ensure that you'll never bonk on a long ride, plan your eating schedule in advance. For rides of 3 hours or more, begin by eating something every 20 minutes. With experience you'll learn whether that's too little or too much and what type of food your body likes best (the longer the ride, the less you'll want to rely on sugar of any type). Once you find a system that serves you well, stick with it.

WEDNESDAY
GOAL: ☐
ROUTE:
DISTANCE/TIME:
WEATHER CONDITIONS:
THOUGHTS:

THURSDAY
GOAL: ☐
ROUTE:
DISTANCE/TIME:
WEATHER CONDITIONS:
THOUGHTS:

FRIDAY

GOAL: ☐

ROUTE:

DISTANCE/TIME:

WEATHER CONDITIONS:

THOUGHTS:

SATURDAY

GOAL: ☐

ROUTE:

DISTANCE/TIME:

WEATHER CONDITIONS:

THOUGHTS:

SUNDAY

GOAL: ☐

ROUTE:

DISTANCE/TIME:

WEATHER CONDITIONS:

THOUGHTS:

WEEKLY TOTAL

TOTAL MILEAGE TO DATE

TIP OF THE WEEK

Triple-Digit Training

Pedal 100 miles in a single day and you've achieved something special. But there can be a big difference between thriving and just surviving on your first century. Your training in the months before the big day should contain a mix of power and endurance. Long, steady rides between 2 and 4 hours build your endurance, whereas short, fast rides give you the power to make it through the tough sections with flying colors.

"You'll never win!"

—Fausto Coppi's mother before his first amateur race in 1938; Coppi would go on to become the greatest Italian cyclist ever, winning the Tour de France, the Tour of Italy, the world professional road championships, and the Hour Record

Ride Your Bike More

Want to get on your bike more frequently? Then get organized. If you know time is short on a given day, pump up your tires, fill your water bottles, and lay out the gear you think you'll need. You'll also want to pick a route and decide on the optimal time to leave. Don't forget to tell your family or coworkers of your plans; once you've made it known that you're going to ride, it'll allow them to plan around it.

MONDAY
GOAL: ☐

ROUTE:

DISTANCE/TIME:

WEATHER CONDITIONS:

THOUGHTS:

TUESDAY
GOAL: ☐

ROUTE:

DISTANCE/TIME:

WEATHER CONDITIONS:

THOUGHTS:

WEDNESDAY
GOAL: ☐

ROUTE:

DISTANCE/TIME:

WEATHER CONDITIONS:

THOUGHTS:

THURSDAY
GOAL: ☐

ROUTE:

DISTANCE/TIME:

WEATHER CONDITIONS:

THOUGHTS:

FRIDAY

GOAL: ☐

ROUTE:

DISTANCE/TIME:

WEATHER CONDITIONS:

THOUGHTS:

SATURDAY

GOAL: ☐

ROUTE:

DISTANCE/TIME:

WEATHER CONDITIONS:

THOUGHTS:

SUNDAY

GOAL: ☐

ROUTE:

DISTANCE/TIME:

WEATHER CONDITIONS:

THOUGHTS:

WEEKLY TOTAL

TOTAL MILEAGE TO DATE

TIP OF THE WEEK

Craving Caffeine?

The coffee or soda you drank on the way to work is wearing off, and you want another hit to get your energy level back up to what feels like normal? Fight it. Swear off the regular soda and opt for the caffeine-free diet variety. Switch to caffeine-free soda and you'll not only break the caffeine/craving connection, but also have more energy—caffeine gives you a false sense of energy.

> "I was utterly heedless about what was happening to my body."

—Casey Patterson, female winner of the Race Across America in 1987, sharing her secret to success

TIP OF THE WEEK

Be Strong of Mind

Don't forget to train your mental muscles in the days just before an event. Try to visualize how you'll ride on the big day. Focus on how much preparation you've done for the ride or race and dream of great success. Don't let uncertainty creep into your mind; be strong. You've done all the work, and racing is your reward. Let the fun begin.

MONDAY

GOAL: ☐

ROUTE:

DISTANCE/TIME:

WEATHER CONDITIONS:

THOUGHTS:

TUESDAY

GOAL: ☐

ROUTE:

DISTANCE/TIME:

WEATHER CONDITIONS:

THOUGHTS:

WEDNESDAY

GOAL: ☐

ROUTE:

DISTANCE/TIME:

WEATHER CONDITIONS:

THOUGHTS:

THURSDAY

GOAL: ☐

ROUTE:

DISTANCE/TIME:

WEATHER CONDITIONS:

THOUGHTS:

FRIDAY

GOAL: ☐

ROUTE:

DISTANCE/TIME:

WEATHER CONDITIONS:

THOUGHTS:

SATURDAY

GOAL: ☐

ROUTE:

DISTANCE/TIME:

WEATHER CONDITIONS:

THOUGHTS:

SUNDAY

GOAL: ☐

ROUTE:

DISTANCE/TIME:

WEATHER CONDITIONS:

THOUGHTS:

WEEKLY TOTAL

TOTAL MILEAGE TO DATE

Breathe Easier

If you are prone to coughing, wheezing, and/or shortness of breath during exercise, you might have exercise-induced asthma (EIA), or exercise-induced bronchospasm (EIB). Not to worry: It's a common and curable condition that occurs in riders of all abilities.

If you have EIA/EIB, you can minimize the chances that it will occur on your next ride by warming up and cooling down thoroughly. You should also limit the intensity of your workouts during times when pollen or air pollution levels are known to be high. Also, if you're going to be exercising in dry, cold air—a major amplifier of EIA/EIB—wear a mask or scarf to buffer your lungs from frosty breaths.

Failing all else, a wide range of medications can be used to fight EIA/EIB. See your physician for testing and recommendations.

> "If you don't know you're going to win in the gate, you're already beat."

—*Shaun Palmer*

Prevent Cramps

Cramps seem to be as much a part of cycling as flat tires and sore backsides. Yet, it doesn't have to be so. Here's how to prevent skeletal muscle cramps on your next ride:

Proper training: Mimicking the intensity, distance, and style of ride that you are preparing for will go a long way in the prevention of cramps.

Adequate hydration: It is known that dehydration causes cramping. Stay adequately hydrated and you should be in the clear.

Electrolyte replacement: Maintaining the proper level of magnesium, potassium, sodium, and chloride in your system is also important in the prevention of cramps.

Stretch regularly: Before and after rides, stretching—although not proven to be a cure-all for cramping—is a good preventive measure.

MONDAY
GOAL: ☐
ROUTE:
DISTANCE/TIME:
WEATHER CONDITIONS:
THOUGHTS:

TUESDAY
GOAL: ☐
ROUTE:
DISTANCE/TIME:
WEATHER CONDITIONS:
THOUGHTS:

WEDNESDAY
GOAL: ☐
ROUTE:
DISTANCE/TIME:
WEATHER CONDITIONS:
THOUGHTS:

THURSDAY
GOAL: ☐
ROUTE:
DISTANCE/TIME:
WEATHER CONDITIONS:
THOUGHTS:

FRIDAY

GOAL: ☐

ROUTE:

DISTANCE/TIME:

WEATHER CONDITIONS:

THOUGHTS:

SATURDAY

GOAL: ☐

ROUTE:

DISTANCE/TIME:

WEATHER CONDITIONS:

THOUGHTS:

SUNDAY

GOAL: ☐

ROUTE:

DISTANCE/TIME:

WEATHER CONDITIONS:

THOUGHTS:

TIP OF THE WEEK

Scout It

Ever notice how much easier a hill is the second time you ride it? If you're focusing on a big event, try to ride as much of the course beforehand as possible. The day before a big century, ride the last 20 miles of the course. You'll feel much more comfortable the next day, having already tackled the hardest part of the course.

WEEKLY TOTAL

TOTAL MILEAGE TO DATE

"I come from farming country, and the people who work the earth have taught me a lot. You plant, you wait for good weather, you harvest. It's a philosophy that has served me well in cycling."

—*Miguel Indurain*

TIP OF THE WEEK

Not a Drag

Riders spend 75 percent of their energy just trying to overcome the forces of wind drag. One very simple way to cut drag during a big event is to carefully pin on your number. Use at least six pins—one each corner and two across the top edge—and fold the number as small as you can without obstructing the information on it.

MONDAY

GOAL: ☐

ROUTE:

DISTANCE/TIME:

WEATHER CONDITIONS:

THOUGHTS:

TUESDAY

GOAL: ☐

ROUTE:

DISTANCE/TIME:

WEATHER CONDITIONS:

THOUGHTS:

WEDNESDAY

GOAL: ☐

ROUTE:

DISTANCE/TIME:

WEATHER CONDITIONS:

THOUGHTS:

THURSDAY

GOAL: ☐

ROUTE:

DISTANCE/TIME:

WEATHER CONDITIONS:

THOUGHTS:

FRIDAY

GOAL: ☐

ROUTE:

DISTANCE/TIME:

WEATHER CONDITIONS:

THOUGHTS:

SATURDAY

GOAL: ☐

ROUTE:

DISTANCE/TIME:

WEATHER CONDITIONS:

THOUGHTS:

SUNDAY

GOAL: ☐

ROUTE:

DISTANCE/TIME:

WEATHER CONDITIONS:

THOUGHTS:

WEEKLY TOTAL

TOTAL MILEAGE TO DATE

Make a Rain Ride Bearable

Almost no one likes riding in the rain. Here's how to make it bearable:

Overdress: Wear more clothes than you think you need, using many layers instead of one or two thick garments. This will allow you to modulate your temperature.

Wear a cap: Riding with a cycling cap under your helmet will help keep you warm, and the brim will help keep road grit from collecting in your eyes.

Ride like you're on ice: To keep the rubber side down, ride carefully. You need more time to turn and stop when the roads are wet. You also need more time to shift, as your drivetrain will not perform as efficiently when soggy.

"I have underperformed compared to my talent, but in some ways it's been a concious decision not to burn myself out."

—British pro David Millar on his lack of big results

Fly Down a Rough Road

When you come to a section of road or trail that is rough or bumpy but still requires you to pedal, shift into a taller gear (actually a smaller rear cog), lift your butt off the saddle slightly, and relax your arms, neck, and shoulders. Shifting into a taller gear will make your entire body more stable, giving you increased control on the less-than-perfect surface. You'll know you've got this technique dialed when you feel like you're floating above the surface instead of having your teeth rattled loose by it.

MONDAY
GOAL: ☐

ROUTE:

DISTANCE/TIME:

WEATHER CONDITIONS:

THOUGHTS:

TUESDAY
GOAL: ☐

ROUTE:

DISTANCE/TIME:

WEATHER CONDITIONS:

THOUGHTS:

WEDNESDAY
GOAL: ☐

ROUTE:

DISTANCE/TIME:

WEATHER CONDITIONS:

THOUGHTS:

THURSDAY
GOAL: ☐

ROUTE:

DISTANCE/TIME:

WEATHER CONDITIONS:

THOUGHTS:

FRIDAY

GOAL: ☐

ROUTE: _____

DISTANCE/TIME: _____

WEATHER CONDITIONS: _____

THOUGHTS: _____

SATURDAY

GOAL: ☐

ROUTE: _____

DISTANCE/TIME: _____

WEATHER CONDITIONS: _____

THOUGHTS: _____

SUNDAY

GOAL: ☐

ROUTE: _____

DISTANCE/TIME: _____

WEATHER CONDITIONS: _____

THOUGHTS: _____

WEEKLY TOTAL

_____

TOTAL MILEAGE TO DATE

_____

TIP OF THE WEEK

Snow Day

When you were a kid, a big snowstorm was the perfect excuse for taking the day off school. As an adult, it's a great chance for you to take a break from your regular training routine. Take a few days off the bike and incorporate into your plan some aerobic exercise such as cross-country skiing or snowshoeing. It'll help you keep your base of fitness in less-than-perfect condition and will give you a mental break from the bike.

"I talk a lot about living through the suffering cycling offers up and how the bad days outnumber the good. But, it's those one or two elusive good days that make it all worth it."

—*Tyler Hamilton after the 2003 Tour de France, where he broke his collarbone in the first week but continued on to win a tough mountain stage*

TIP OF THE WEEK

Got Pain?

Before you pop a few pain-relieving pills, decide whether you're just treating pain or whether swelling is also an issue. For pain alone, acetaminophen is great, but for pain with swelling try something with asprin or ibuprofen, which fights both.

MONDAY
GOAL: ☐
ROUTE:
DISTANCE/TIME:
WEATHER CONDITIONS:
THOUGHTS:

TUESDAY
GOAL: ☐
ROUTE:
DISTANCE/TIME:
WEATHER CONDITIONS:
THOUGHTS:

WEDNESDAY
GOAL: ☐
ROUTE:
DISTANCE/TIME:
WEATHER CONDITIONS:
THOUGHTS:

THURSDAY
GOAL: ☐
ROUTE:
DISTANCE/TIME:
WEATHER CONDITIONS:
THOUGHTS:

FRIDAY

GOAL: ☐

ROUTE:

DISTANCE/TIME:

WEATHER CONDITIONS:

THOUGHTS:

SATURDAY

GOAL: ☐

ROUTE:

DISTANCE/TIME:

WEATHER CONDITIONS:

THOUGHTS:

SUNDAY

GOAL: ☐

ROUTE:

DISTANCE/TIME:

WEATHER CONDITIONS:

THOUGHTS:

WEEKLY TOTAL

TOTAL MILEAGE TO DATE

Stop on a Dime

Everyone should know how to make a panic stop, especially those riders who live and train in an urban environment.

To make a panic stop, firmly apply both brakes, putting more emphasis on the front (it supplies 75 percent of your total stopping power). If the road is wet or full of gravel or another hazard, use your brakes in equal parts to ensure that the front wheel doesn't slide or push out from under you. As you apply the brakes, shift your weight back, straightening your arms and shooting your butt off the back of the saddle if necessary. This will counteract the tendency of your bike to pivot on the front wheel or endo.

"If you can
pedal, you
carry on."

—David Millar

Climb More Efficiently

One of the big secrets to Lance Armstrong's Tour de France success is that he learned how to climb more efficiently. For Armstrong this means climbing while seated except for the moments when he's staging an attack. Staying seated results in a lower heart rate for a given speed and thus conserves energy. You should stand only when the climb becomes suddenly steep or you need to make a hard acceleration. On long climbs (3 miles or more) you may want to stand periodically to stretch your muscles and enhance circulation.

MONDAY

GOAL:

ROUTE:

DISTANCE/TIME:

WEATHER CONDITIONS:

THOUGHTS:

TUESDAY

GOAL:

ROUTE:

DISTANCE/TIME:

WEATHER CONDITIONS:

THOUGHTS:

WEDNESDAY

GOAL:

ROUTE:

DISTANCE/TIME:

WEATHER CONDITIONS:

THOUGHTS:

THURSDAY

GOAL:

ROUTE:

DISTANCE/TIME:

WEATHER CONDITIONS:

THOUGHTS:

FRIDAY

GOAL: ☐

ROUTE:

DISTANCE/TIME:

WEATHER CONDITIONS:

THOUGHTS:

SATURDAY

GOAL: ☐

ROUTE:

DISTANCE/TIME:

WEATHER CONDITIONS:

THOUGHTS:

SUNDAY

GOAL: ☐

ROUTE:

DISTANCE/TIME:

WEATHER CONDITIONS:

THOUGHTS:

WEEKLY TOTAL

TOTAL MILEAGE TO DATE

TIP OF THE WEEK

Become an Incredible Sprinter and Even Better Bike Handler

Riding and racing on one of the 20 velodromes in the United States will fine-tune your sprint, buff up your muscles, and hone your bike handling. With no brakes and only one gear, training and racing on the track is a time-honored method for rounding out a racer's fitness and skills, but it can help anyone become a better cyclist. To find a velodrome close to you, check the Fixed Gear Fever Web site, www.fixedgearfever.com.

NOW WHAT?

THERE'S AN ENTIRE YEAR OF EXPERIENCE IN THIS LOG. WHAT CAN IT TELL YOU?

Welcome to the end of your *Bicycling Training Journal*. Have you spent the past year compiling a detailed riding log? Did you record a lot of hard numbers? Or did you concentrate on how riding made you feel and where you'd like to ride in the future?

No matter what you've chronicled, it'd be a pity to stick the journal on a shelf or file it away when you could be using it to plot your riding plans and goals for next year. Sift through these pages. Learn what type of riding is important to you. You'll find it easier to set attainable goals and build resolve when you study where you've been and what you've done.

Here are a few pointers for using your completed journal to boost next year's performance:

1 Look back at the best rides of the year. What made them so incredible? Was it the location? A particular group of riding partners? A certain distance? Try to trace a common thread through your great riding experiences and repeat them in the future.

2 Try to discover what time of day your body responds the best to exercise. We all have a few hours every day when our body performs at its peak. Figure out when that is, and try to get out on your bike during that time.

3 In reviewing your journal, you'll remember rides that you loved and wonder "Why didn't I do them more often?" Find three rides that worked for you, and pencil them into your journal for next year.

4 Sift through the data, and find the month when you were able to ride the greatest number of hours. What was working for you? Were you buckling down and making time to ride? Was it that there was more daylight? Was it a slow time at work? Discover and exploit your peak performance seasons.

NOW WHAT?

5 Review the periods that you rode the least. What was keeping you from getting out more? Was it a major life event or simply a time management issue? Is there a way that you can better organize your life to make more time for riding?

6 Did you suffer any hard-to-explain injuries last year? Your diary will probably contain clues to the origin of your problem. Was it that you rode too hard when you were lacking fitness? Did a seemingly small injury lead to bigger problems? Was it the result of stress and exhaustion?

7 Based on what you've logged in your journal and the memories it stirs, make a plan for the coming year. Include short-term goals (such as a day of the week that you'll always make time to ride) and longer-term dreams (an event that you want to focus on, a cycling-oriented vacation, et cetera).

8 Based on the experience reflected in your journal, pick rides, races, or other events that you want to enter next year. Perhaps it's an event where you've done well and want to repeat that performance. Maybe it's something you've always dreamed of doing, like a 24-hour race or a double century.

EQUIPMENT LOG

GEAR I USED THIS YEAR AND WHY.

You pop into a bike shop for a tube and a couple of energy bars and walk out $9 lighter. No big deal, right? What if we told you that the average enthusiast spends nearly $3,000 on inner tubes alone over a lifetime of cycling? What if we told you that same person spends $11,000 on energy food? What if we gave you the grand total: a whopping $121,253 spent on equipment over the average cyclist's life on two wheels?

You'd probably want to find a way to keep track of your purchases. We've provided the spaces below for that reason. As with the rest of this training journal, be sure to include as much information as possible—you never know which mundane detail might save you thousands of dollars in the long run.

ITEM

DATE PURCHASED

PURCHASED FROM

PRICE PAID

SIZE

FEATURES

OVERALL IMPRESSION

WOULD YOU PURCHASE THIS AGAIN?

ITEM

DATE PURCHASED

PURCHASED FROM

PRICE PAID

SIZE

FEATURES

OVERALL IMPRESSION

WOULD YOU PURCHASE THIS AGAIN?

EQUIPMENT LOG

ITEM

DATE PURCHASED

PURCHASED FROM

PRICE PAID

SIZE

FEATURES

OVERALL IMPRESSION

WOULD YOU PURCHASE THIS AGAIN?

ITEM

DATE PURCHASED

PURCHASED FROM

PRICE PAID

SIZE

FEATURES

OVERALL IMPRESSION

WOULD YOU PURCHASE THIS AGAIN?

ITEM

DATE PURCHASED

PURCHASED FROM

PRICE PAID

SIZE

FEATURES

OVERALL IMPRESSION

WOULD YOU PURCHASE THIS AGAIN?

EQUIPMENT LOG

ITEM

DATE PURCHASED

PURCHASED FROM

PRICE PAID

SIZE

FEATURES

OVERALL IMPRESSION

WOULD YOU PURCHASE THIS AGAIN?

ITEM

DATE PURCHASED

PURCHASED FROM

PRICE PAID

SIZE

FEATURES

OVERALL IMPRESSION

WOULD YOU PURCHASE THIS AGAIN?

ITEM

DATE PURCHASED

PURCHASED FROM

PRICE PAID

SIZE

FEATURES

OVERALL IMPRESSION

WOULD YOU PURCHASE THIS AGAIN?

EQUIPMENT LOG

ITEM

DATE PURCHASED

PURCHASED FROM

PRICE PAID

SIZE

FEATURES

OVERALL IMPRESSION

WOULD YOU PURCHASE THIS AGAIN?

ITEM

DATE PURCHASED

PURCHASED FROM

PRICE PAID

SIZE

FEATURES

OVERALL IMPRESSION

WOULD YOU PURCHASE THIS AGAIN?

ITEM

DATE PURCHASED

PURCHASED FROM

PRICE PAID

SIZE

FEATURES

OVERALL IMPRESSION

WOULD YOU PURCHASE THIS AGAIN?

RAVE RIDES

TWO-WHEELED TRIPS I'LL ALWAYS REMEMBER.

Maybe you rode your first century, or tackled the toughest road of your life, finishing bruised and exhausted but wearing a gold medal. Or maybe a casual outing with your buddies stretched into a 12-hour epic.

There's no telling how many "all-time greatest rides" you'll have this year, but it's certain you'll want to remember them. That's why we've included this section. Throughout the year, take notes on the things you did and the things you learned. Did a mid-September ride find you powering up hills that might have seemed impossible just a month before? Write it down. Did you get the best of a buddy who has always gotten the better of you? Put it in here. The more details you include, the more memories you'll enjoy in years to come.

RIDE NAME

DATE

RIDING PARTNERS

DISTANCE

LENGTH OF TIME

START LOCATION

ROUTE DESCRIPTION

BIGGEST CHALLENGE

MOST MEMORABLE MOMENT

RIDE NAME

DATE

RIDING PARTNERS

DISTANCE

LENGTH OF TIME

RAVE RIDES

START LOCATION

ROUTE DESCRIPTION

BIGGEST CHALLENGE

MOST MEMORABLE MOMENT

RIDE NAME

DATE

RIDING PARTNERS

DISTANCE

LENGTH OF TIME

START LOCATION

ROUTE DESCRIPTION

BIGGEST CHALLENGE

MOST MEMORABLE MOMENT

RIDE NAME

DATE

RIDING PARTNERS

DISTANCE

LENGTH OF TIME

START LOCATION

ROUTE DESCRIPTION

BIGGEST CHALLENGE

MOST MEMORABLE MOMENT

RAVE RIDES

RIDE NAME

DATE

RIDING PARTNERS

DISTANCE

LENGTH OF TIME

START LOCATION

ROUTE DESCRIPTION

BIGGEST CHALLENGE

MOST MEMORABLE MOMENT

RIDE NAME

DATE

RIDING PARTNERS

DISTANCE

LENGTH OF TIME

START LOCATION

ROUTE DESCRIPTION

BIGGEST CHALLENGE

MOST MEMORABLE MOMENT

RIDE NAME

DATE

RIDING PARTNERS

DISTANCE

LENGTH OF TIME

RAVE RIDES

START LOCATION

ROUTE DESCRIPTION

BIGGEST CHALLENGE

MOST MEMORABLE MOMENT

RIDE NAME

DATE

RIDING PARTNERS

DISTANCE

LENGTH OF TIME

START LOCATION

ROUTE DESCRIPTION

BIGGEST CHALLENGE

MOST MEMORABLE MOMENT

RIDE NAME

DATE

RIDING PARTNERS

DISTANCE

LENGTH OF TIME

START LOCATION

ROUTE DESCRIPTION

BIGGEST CHALLENGE

MOST MEMORABLE MOMENT

BIKE FIT BASICS

BECAUSE A BIKE THAT DOESN'T FIT IS NO BIKE AT ALL.

The lightest, flashiest, snazziest bike in the world is useless if it doesn't meet your needs. Yep, finding a riding position with a precise balance of comfort and power is the single most important thing you can do to ensure two-wheeled bliss.

Proper bike fit is a process that is continually in flux, and from one season to the next you'll find that you need to make slight alterations in your position. Use the information below to get close to your ideal position, and continue to refine your position from there.

SEAT

Height: Theories vary on the correct calculation for seat height, but most experts agree that your leg should be nearly straight but not locked or stretched as you hit the bottom of the pedal stroke. A more scientific way to generate a beginning number for the distance between the top of your saddle and the platform of your pedal is to carefully measure your inseam and multiply it by 0.883.

Fore and Aft: Sitting on your bike, pedal backward a few rotations, and stop with your cranks parallel to the ground. Drop a plumb line (a weighted string) from the bony bump just below your kneecap down to your foot. In the proper position, it should sit on top of the pedal axle or be less than 5 mm fore or aft of it.

Angle: With your bike on a flat surface, use a small level to determine an absolutely level position for the saddle. Experiment from there. A very slight tilt in either direction can dramatically alter the pressure you feel as you sit.

BIKE FIT BASICS

HANDLEBAR

Height and Reach: The rule of thumb for handlebar reach on a road bike is that your arms should form a 90-degree angle with your torso when your hands are on the hoods. Mountain bike riders should be positioned so that there is less room between their torso and arms.

Width: Handlebar width is directly related to shoulder width. Road cyclists choose a bar that is as wide as their shoulders, measured as the distance between the bony bumps on the outside top of the shoulder joints. Mountain bike riders should select a bar that suits the terrain they ride most often—go narrow for singletrack, wider for fire roads.

Angle: Whether mountain or road, this is nearly all personal choice. Start with a neutral position and experiment from there. During your experiment, don't just change the angle of your bar, change the angle and position of your controls.

CLEATS

Fore and Aft: Your cleats should be mounted so that the pedal spindles sit directly under the ball of your foot.

Lateral: Riders who are using clipless pedals for the first time should be sure to use a system with cleats that have float. This allows the heel of the foot to swivel both in and out, allowing you to find the best lateral alignment for your foot.

BIKE SETUP RECORD

CONSIDER THIS YOUR LITTLE BLACK BOOK OF BICYCLING.

We've all had our great loves, but ultimately bikes come and bikes go. Before you know it, the Trek you doted on last season will be collecting dust in your garage, and you'll be cranking out the miles on a sleek and sexy Litespeed. Eventually, you'll sell that one and buy a dream bike with a more exotic pedigree. A little Italian number perhaps? On and on, the cycle of cycles continues.

Once your current bike is perfectly configured, we suggest that you use these pages to record as much information about it as possible. Not only will this make the transition to a new bike easier, but also it'll help in 5 or 6 years when you're dreaming wistfully of the way your old Litespeed fit. When that day comes, you'll have the precise geometry and spec of your old machine. Just dial up those old numbers and voilà: Your love is rekindled.

If you're new to the sport or have never felt comfortable on your bike, take the time to go to the shop in your area with the best reputation for professional bike fitting. Like finding the right tailor, being positioned by a professional will make you more comfortable and save you the cost (and embarrassment) of buying a bike that doesn't fit.

FRAMESET

FRAME

FORK

SEAT TUBE

TOP TUBE

SEAT ANGLE

HEAD ANGLE

FORK RAKE

CHAINSTAYS

FRONT CENTER MEASUREMENT FROM BOTTOM BRACKET TO FRONT AXLE

BOTTOM BRACKET HEIGHT (FROM GROUND TO THE CENTER OF THE BOTTOM BRACKET)

BIKE SETUP RECORD

COMPONENTS

SEAT

SEATPOST

STEM LENGTH   CM

HANDLEBARS   WIDTH   CM

HEADSET

SHIFTERS

BRAKE LEVERS

BRAKE CALIPERS

FRONT DERAILLEUR

REAR DERAILLEUR

CHAIN

CASSETTE   TEETH

CRANK   LENGTH   MM   TEETH

BOTTOM BRACKET

HUBS

RIMS

TIRES

TUBES

ACCESSORIES (BOTTLE CAGES, COMPUTER, ET CETERA)

PHOTO CREDITS

Page 4: **Corbis Tempsport/CORBIS**

Pages 5, 15, 34, 74: **Mike Powell/ALLSPORT**

Pages 7, 40, 75: **Hilmar**

Pages 8, 31, 59, 73, 95: **Mitch Mandel**

Pages 9, 13, 17, 29, 69, 88, 89: **John Hamel**

Pages 10, 23, 25: **Photodisc Green/Getty Images**

Page 11: **Annie Griffiths Belt/CORBIS**

Page 14: **Stone/Getty Images**

Pages 16, 103: **Photodisc**

Pages 19, 37, 39, 45, 47, 65, 71, 93, 101: **Royalty-Free/CORBIS**

Page 20: **Pascal Rondeau/ALLSPORT**

Pages 21, 49, 83: **Photodisc Red/Getty Images**

Page 22: **Tim Davis/CORBIS**

Page 26 (top): **Austrian Archives/CORBIS**

Pages 26 (bottom), 77, 87, 91: **Rodale Images**

Pages 27, 38, 41, 81: **Kurt Wilson**

Pages 28, 57: **Hughes Martin/CORBIS**

Pages 30, 80, 82: **Robert Laberge/ALLSPORT**

Pages 33, 107: **Digital Vision/Getty Images**

Page 35: **Tom Bean/CORBIS**

Page 36: **Allsport UK/ALLSPORT**

Page 43: **Tim Pannell/CORBIS**

Page 46: **Bettman/CORBIS**

Pages 48, 53, 85, 99: **Photodisc Blue/Getty Images**

Page 51: **Simon Cudby**

Page 55: **Mark A. Johnson/CORBIS**

Page 56: **Hulton-Deutsch Collection/CORBIS**

Page 61: **Joseph Cultice**

Page 67: **Helen King/CORBIS**

Page 72: **Conde Nast Archive/CORBIS**

Page 76: **Images.com/Getty Images**

Page 79: **Dough Pensinger/ALLSPORT**

Page 84: **Margaret Skronvanek**

Page 94: **David Stoecklein/CORBIS**

Page 96: **Shelley Gazin/CORBIS**

Page 105: **Karl Weatherly/CORBIS**

Page 106: **ALLSPORT**